W9-AAI-877

DATE DUE

GAYLORD   PRINTED IN U.S.A.

ACE YOUR SCIENCE PROJECT USING CHEMISTRY MAGIC AND TOYS

Titles in the
ACE YOUR SCIENCE PROJECT series:

Ace Your Chemistry Science Project:
Great Science Fair Ideas

ISBN-13: 978-0-7660-3227-9
ISBN-10:   0-7660-3227-2

Ace Your Ecology and
Environmental Science Project:
Great Science Fair Ideas

ISBN-13: 978-0-7660-3216-3
ISBN-10:   0-7660-3216-7

Ace Your Food Science Project:
Great Science Fair Ideas

ISBN-13: 978-0-7660-3228-6
ISBN-10:   0-7660-3228-0

Ace Your Science Project Using
Chemistry Magic and Toys:
Great Science Fair Ideas

ISBN-13: 978-0-7660-3226-2
ISBN-10:   0-7660-3226-4

Ace Your Space Science Project:
Great Science Fair Ideas

ISBN-13: 978-0-7660-3230-9
ISBN-10:   0-7660-3230-2

A+ ACE YOUR SCIENCE PROJECT

ACE YOUR SCIENCE PROJECT USING CHEMISTRY MAGIC AND TOYS

Robert Gardner

GREAT SCIENCE FAIR IDEAS

E **Enslow Publishers, Inc.**
40 Industrial Road
Box 398
Berkeley Heights, NJ 07922
USA

http://www.enslow.com

Library of Congress Cataloging-in-Publication Data

Gardner, Robert, 1929–
Ace your science project using chemistry magic and toys : great science fair ideas / Robert Gardner.
    p. cm. — (Ace your science project)
    Summary: "Presents several fun science experiments and project ideas using toys and chemistry
    magic"—Provided by publisher.
    Includes bibliographical references and index.
    ISBN-13: 978-0-7660-3226-2
    1. Chemistry—Experiments—Juvenile literature. 2. Toys—Experiments—Juvenile literature.
    3. Science projects—Juvenile literature. 4. Science fairs—Juvenile literature. I. Title.
    QD38.G345 2009
    540.78—dc22

                     2008004685

Printed in the United States of America
052010 Lake Book Manufacturing, Inc., Melrose Park, IL
10 9 8 7 6 5 4 3 2

ISBN-10: 0-7660-3226-4

To Our Readers: We have done our best to make sure all Internet Addresses in this book were active and appropriate when we went to press. However, the author and the publisher have no control over and assume no liability for the material available on those Internet sites or on other Web sites they may link to. Any comments or suggestions can be sent by e-mail to comments@enslow.com or to the address on the back cover.

♻ Enslow Publishers, Inc., is committed to printing our books on recycled paper. The paper in every book contains 10% to 30% post-consumer waste (PCW). The cover board on the outside of each book contains 100% PCW. Our goal is to do our part to help young people and the environment too!

The experiments in this book are a collection of Robert Gardner's best experiments, which were previously published by Enslow Publishers, Inc. in *Science Project Ideas About Kitchen Chemistry*, *Science Project Ideas in the House*, *Science Projects About Physics in the Home*, *Science Projects About the Physics of Sports*, *Science Projects About the Physics of Toys and Games*, and *Science Projects About the Science Behind Magic*.

Illustration Credits: Enslow Publishers, Inc., Figures 1, 3, 5, 6, 12, 13, 18, 20, 21, 23, 24; Gary Koellhoffer, Figure 10; Stefanie Rowland, Figures 25–30; Stephen F. Delisle, Figures 2, 4, 7–9, 11, 14, 15–17, 19, 22.

Photo Credits: Shutterstock

Cover Photos: Shutterstock

CONTENTS

CHAPTER 1

There Is Magic in the Air   13

CHAPTER 2

Magic Through Chemistry   35

◎ **Experiments marked with this symbol contain material that might be used for a science fair project.**

○ *Experiments marked with this symbol contain material that might be used for a science fair project.*

INTRODUCTION

When you hear the word *science*, do you think of a person in a white lab coat surrounded by beakers of bubbling liquids, specialized lab equipment, and computers? What exactly is science? Maybe you think science is only a subject you learn in school. Science is much more than this.

Science is the study of the things that are all around you, every day. No matter where you are or what you are doing, scientific principles are at work. You don't need special materials or equipment, or even a white lab coat, to be a scientist. Materials commonly found in your home, at school, or at a local store will allow you to become a scientist and pursue an area of interest. By making careful observations and asking questions about how things work, you can begin to design your own experiments.

Perhaps you are reading this book because you are looking for an idea for a science fair project for school, or maybe you are just hoping to find something fun to do on a rainy day. This book will provide an opportunity for you to perform chemical magic tricks, build toys, and do some experiments at your local playground. For all of the experiments, you will discover the science behind what you are doing. You may be surprised that you can have fun and learn science at the same time. You can entertain others with the magic tricks described in this book. Along the way, you will learn about chemistry and physics.

SCIENCE FAIR PROJECT IDEAS

Many of the experiments in this book may be appropriate for science fair projects. These experiments are marked with a symbol ( ) and include a section called Science Fair Project Ideas. The ideas in this section will provide suggestions to help you develop your own original science fair project. However, judges at such fairs do not reward projects or experiments that are simply copied from a book. For example, a model of a toy car, which is commonly found at these fairs, would probably not impress judges unless it was done in a novel or creative way. On the other hand, a carefully performed experiment to find out how the angle of incline affects the car's speed would be likely to receive careful consideration.

THE SCIENTIFIC METHOD

All scientists look at the world and try to understand how things work. They make careful observations and conduct research about a question. Different areas of science use different approaches. Depending on the phenomenon being investigated, one method is likely to be more appropriate than another. Designing a new medication for heart disease, studying the spread of an invasive plant species such as purple loosestrife, and finding evidence that there was once water on Mars all require different methods.

Despite the differences, however, all scientists use a similar general approach to do experiments. It is called the scientific method. In most experiments, some or all of the following steps are used: making an observation, formulating a question, making a hypothesis (an answer to the question) and prediction (an if-then statement), designing and conducting an experiment, analyzing results and drawing conclusions, and accepting or rejecting the hypothesis. Scientists then share their findings with others by writing articles that are published in journals. After—and only after—a hypothesis has repeatedly been supported by experiments can it be considered a theory.

You might be wondering how to get an experiment started. When you observe something in the world, you may become curious and think of a question. Your question can be answered by a well-designed investigation. Your question may also arise from an earlier experiment or from background reading. Once you have a question, you should make a hypothesis. Your hypothesis is a possible answer to the question (what you think will happen). Once you have a hypothesis, it is time to design an experiment.

In some cases, it is appropriate to do a controlled experiment. This means there are two groups treated exactly the same except for the single factor that you are testing. That factor is often called a variable. For example, if you want to investigate whether raisins will rise to the surface when placed in a carbonated beverage, two groups may be used. One group is called the control group, and the other is called the experimental group. The two groups should be treated exactly the same: The same number of raisins should be placed in the same amount of liquid, be kept at the same temperature, and so forth. The control group will be the raisins placed in sugar water, while the experimental group will be the raisins placed in ginger ale. The variable is carbonation. It is the thing that changes, and it is the only difference between the two groups.

During the experiment, you will collect data. For example, you might count the number of raisins that rise to the surface. You might time how long it takes for the raisins to rise. By comparing the data collected from the control group with the data collected from the experimental group, you will draw conclusions. Since the two groups were treated exactly alike, all the raisins in the ginger ale rising to the surface would allow you to conclude with confidence that it is a result of the one thing that was different: carbonation.

Two other terms that are often used in scientific experiments are *dependent* and *independent* variables. One dependent variable here is the rising of raisins, because it depends upon carbonation. Carbonation is the independent variable (it doesn't depend on anything). After the data is collected, it is analyzed to see whether the hypothesis was supported or rejected. Often, the results of one experiment will lead you to a related question, or they may send you off in a different direction. Whatever the results, there is something to be learned from all scientific experiments.

SCIENCE FAIRS

Science fair judges tend to reward creative thought and imagination. However, it is difficult to be creative or imaginative unless you are really interested in your project. If you decide to do a project, be sure to choose a topic that appeals to you. Consider, too, your own ability and the cost of materials. Don't pursue a project that you can't afford.

If you decide to use a project found in this book for a science fair, you will need to find ways to modify or extend it. This should not be difficult because you will probably find that as you do these projects new ideas for experiments will come to mind. These new experiments could make excellent science fair projects, particularly because they spring from your own mind and are interesting to you.

If you decide to enter a science fair and have never done so before, you should read some of the books listed in the Further Reading section. The books that deal specifically with science fairs will provide plenty of helpful hints and lots of useful information that will enable you to avoid the pitfalls that sometimes plague first-time entrants. You will learn how to prepare appealing reports that include charts and graphs, how to set up and display your work, how to present your project, and how to relate to judges and visitors.

SAFETY FIRST

As with many activities, safety is important in science, and certain rules apply when conducting experiments. Some of the rules below may seem obvious to you, but each is important to follow.

1. Have **an adult** help you whenever the book advises.

2. Wear eye protection and closed-toe shoes (rather than sandals), and tie back long hair.

3. Don't eat or drink while doing experiments, and never taste substances being used.

4. Avoid touching chemicals.

5. Keep flammable substances away from fire.

6. Do only those experiments that are described in the book or those that have been approved by **an adult**.

7. Never engage in horseplay or play practical jokes.

8. Before beginning, read through the entire experimental procedure to make sure you understand all instructions, and clear all items from your work space.

9. At the end of every activity, clean all materials used and put them away. Wash your hands thoroughly with soap and water.

Chapter 1

There Is Magic in the Air

THROUGHOUT THIS CHAPTER, the activities are written as if you will be performing your science "magic" before an audience. You may, of course, do some of these experiments in front of friends, relatives, classmates, elementary school classes, or other audiences. If you do, you will want to rehearse your act before making any public presentations. On the other hand, you may prefer to do these experiments by yourself simply because you can learn more about science in a way that is entertaining. Whatever your approach, enjoy doing the experiments and discovering a lot about science.

At the end of many experiments in Chapters 1 and 2, you will find a section entitled "The Science Behind the Magic," which explains the scientific principles involved in what may appear to be magic. If you do these experiments as parts of a "Science Through Magic" act, you may or may not choose to share this information with your audience.

The projects in this chapter are all related to the pressure exerted by the air that makes up Earth's atmosphere. Because air has no color or odor and has a very low density (about 1.2 grams per liter), we are often unaware of its presence. Despite the fact that air weighs only about 1/1,000 as much as an equal volume of water, it forms a "sea" more than 100 kilometers (60 miles) deep. Since we live at the bottom of this sea of air, the air pushes on every square centimeter of us and everything else on the surface of the earth with a force of about 10 newtons (N). (A newton is a unit used in measuring force; 1.0 N is equal to 0.22 pounds.) The pressure of the air is 10 newtons per square centimeter (N/cm^2), or 14.6 pounds per square inch (lb/in^2).

To get a sense of how large this pressure is, consider the palm of your outstretched hand. It is probably about 7.5 cm (3 in) wide and 7.5 cm long. Its area, therefore, is about 56 cm^2. You would have to hold 560 newtons (about 125 pounds) in your palm to have a pressure equal to the amount of pressure the atmosphere puts on your hand.

You may wonder, then, how you can possibly raise your hand as easily as you do. The reason is that the air is pushing upward on your hand (and the rest of your body) with forces that are as large as those pushing downward. Air is made up of tiny molecules, far too small to see, that are all in constant motion. They collide with you and with everything else in contact with air. Like anything that bumps into you, they exert a force on you. Because they are moving in all directions, they exert as much push on the bottom of your hand as they do on the top.

The activities in this chapter will help make you more aware of air and the pressure it exerts on everything it touches.

1.1 A Balloon in a Bottle

Materials:
-2 balloons
-½- or 1-liter (pint or quart) soda bottle
-plastic drinking straw

Place a balloon inside a 1-liter soda bottle, as shown in Figure 1a. Leave the mouth of the balloon outside the bottle so you can blow into it. If you do this as part of a science magic show, invite a member of your audience to try to blow up the balloon. The person will find it impossible to do.

Remove the balloon and insert a plastic drinking straw into the bottle. Put a new balloon (to avoid transferring any germs from the first balloon) into the bottle (see Figure 1b). You can now fill the bottle with the balloon by blowing air into the balloon.

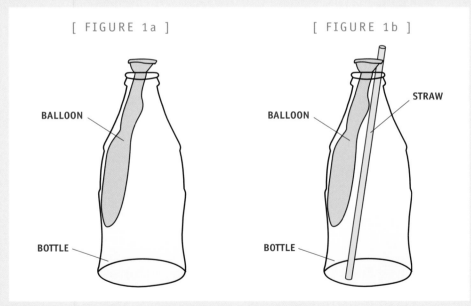

[FIGURE 1a]

[FIGURE 1b]

BALLOON

BOTTLE

BALLOON

STRAW

BOTTLE

1a) It is impossible to blow up the balloon in the bottle. b) Adding a straw makes it possible to blow up the balloon because air can now escape from the bottle as it is compressed by the expanding balloon.

THE SCIENCE BEHIND THE MAGIC

The straw allows air to escape from the bottle as it is replaced by the air you blow into the balloon. Without the straw, the balloon quickly seals the mouth of the bottle. As a result, no air can escape. The pressure exerted by the trapped air inside the bottle, around the balloon, becomes compressed. Soon the pressure of this trapped air becomes greater than the pressure the person from the audience can exert by blowing into the balloon.

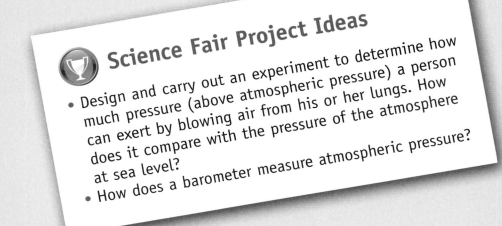

Science Fair Project Ideas

- Design and carry out an experiment to determine how much pressure (above atmospheric pressure) a person can exert by blowing air from his or her lungs. How does it compare with the pressure of the atmosphere at sea level?
- How does a barometer measure atmospheric pressure?

1.2 A Funnel That Will Not Empty

Materials:
- plastic funnel
- one-hole rubber stopper: hole should match size of funnel's spout
- flask or bottle, about 250 mL (1/2 pint)
- water colored with food coloring
- container to hold water

If you punch a hole below the water level in the side of a water-filled can, water will flow out of the can. The pressure of the air and the column of water above the hole is greater than the pressure of the air alone outside the hole. Water always flows from higher pressure to lower pressure.

To begin this bit of science magic, insert the spout of a plastic funnel through the hole of a one-hole rubber stopper. Place the stopper loosely into the neck of a flask or bottle. Hold the rubber stopper so that it remains loose in the neck of the flask or bottle as you pour a small amount of colored water from another container into the funnel. Your audience should be able to see the water flowing into the flask or bottle. Empty the water back into its original container.

While you are emptying the water, use your hand, out of sight of the audience, to push the stopper firmly into the mouth of the flask. Now invite someone from the audience to pour the water into the funnel. This time the water will remain in the funnel, as shown in Figure 2a. Very little water will enter the flask or bottle. Again, empty the water back into its original container.

Finally, remove the stopper and funnel from the flask and pour most of the water into the flask. Then insert the stopper and funnel tightly into the neck of the flask, and turn the apparatus upside down, as shown in Figure 2b. Very little water will escape; most of it will remain in the flask.

If someone thinks you have plugged the funnel's spout, turn the apparatus upright and remove the funnel and stopper. Show them that the funnel's spout is open by letting some water flow through it. Put the stopper firmly into the bottle or flask and turn it upside down again. The water again will remain in the flask.

THE SCIENCE BEHIND THE MAGIC

When the funnel is above the flask and the stopper is loose, air can escape from the flask as it is replaced by water pouring through the funnel. When the stopper is firmly in the mouth of the flask, air cannot escape. The water that enters the funnel compresses the air below it enough to make the pressure inside the flask equal to the pressure of the air and the small column of water in the funnel. Since pressures are equal, water will not flow through the funnel.

When you turn the funnel and flask upside down, a few drops of water enter the funnel. This increases the volume of air trapped above the water, which lowers the pressure of the air. Since the pressure of the air beneath the funnel is equal to the pressure of the air and water above, the water remains in the flask. Allow more air into the flask by placing a straw in the funnel, and water will flow out.

FUNNEL

WATER

ONE-HOLE
STOPPER

FLASK

[FIGURE 2b]

WATER

ONE-HOLE
STOPPER

FUNNEL

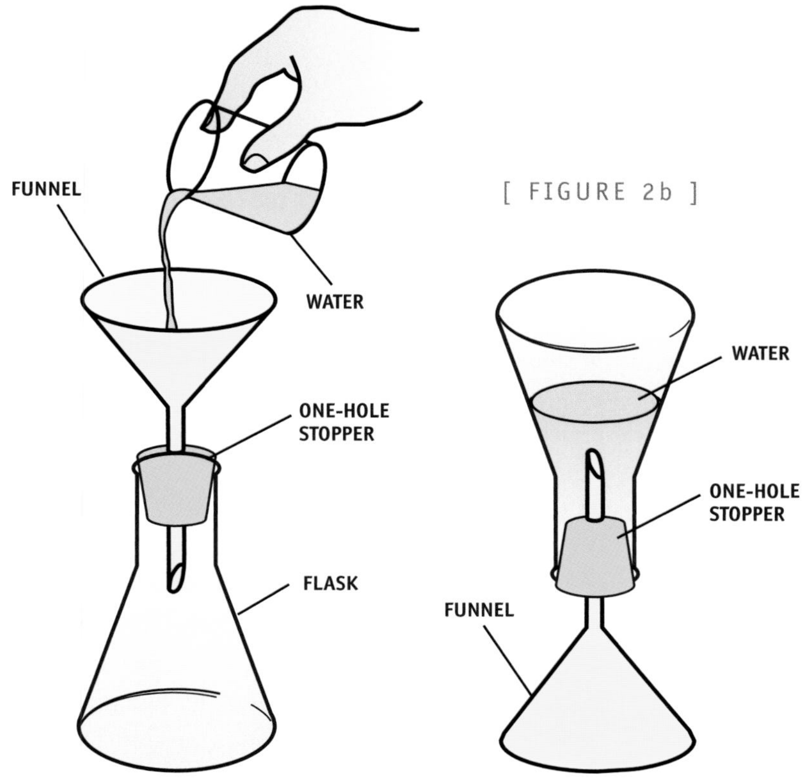

2a) As long as the stopper is snugly in the neck of the flask, water cannot flow from the funnel into the flask. b) With the stopper firmly in the neck of the flask, water cannot empty through the funnel from the flask.

Materials:
- plastic bottle with screw-on cap
- pail of water
- another person
- nail

Submerge a plastic bottle in a pail of water. When the bottle is full of water, screw on its cap and remove it from the pail. Hold the bottle up so that the audience can see that it is full and not leaking. Then ask someone from the audience to hold the bottle. When you hand it to the person, water will begin to leak from the bottom of the bottle. Take the bottle back and the water immediately stops.

THE SCIENCE BEHIND THE MAGIC

The reason the bottle does not leak when it is in your hand is not because you have a magic touch, but because you know *where* to touch. Before the show, use a nail to punch two holes in the bottle—one in the bottom and one in the side near the top, as shown in Figure 3.

When you remove the bottle from the pail, put one of your fingers over the hole near the top of the bottle. After a few drops of water fall out of the bottom hole, the bottle will stop leaking. After a few drops fall from the bottom hole, the volume of the air trapped inside the bottle above the water increases. This reduces the pressure of the trapped air until it is less than the air pressure outside the bottle. Since the pressure of the air on the outside of the hole is greater than the pressure of the air and water above the hole, the water remains in the bottle. Once you remove your finger, the air above the water is exposed to the outside air, and air pressure forces more air into the space at the top of the bottle. The pressure at the bottom of the bottle is now greater than the air pressure outside it, so water will flow from the bottle.

When the top hole is open, can you explain why the pressure at the bottom of the bottle is greater than the air pressure outside the bottle?

[FIGURE 3]

HOLE NEAR TOP OF BOTTLE

HOLE IN BOTTOM OF BOTTLE

The "magic" bottle will only work if two holes are made in it.

Materials:

- an adult

- suction cup: buy one about 4.5 cm (1.75 in) in diameter at a hardware store

- card from a deck of playing cards

- drill

Remove any hooks or other devices that may be attached to the suction cup. **Ask an adult** to drill a small hole through the center of the cup. Place the cup on a playing card and press down, covering the hole in the cup with your index finger. Then lift the cup and card together from the table. If you want to add a little showmanship to the act, rub the card a few times and say a few magic words before you lift it.

Then invite someone from the audience to lift the card in the same way. It is not likely that they will be able to do so.

THE SCIENCE BEHIND THE MAGIC

When you place the suction cup on the card, cover the hole in the center of the cup with your index finger and then press down. As you press down, you will squeeze some air from the cup. As you pick up the cup, it begins to spring back to its original shape. As a result, the pressure of the trapped air in the cup becomes less than the pressure of the air in the room. Keeping the hole covered with your finger maintains that low pressure. The air pressure below the card is now greater than the pressure of the air in the cup above the card. Consequently, air pressure holds the card against the cup. If you remove your finger, air will enter the cup, the pressure inside the cup will become equal to the air pressure, and the card will fall.

Pressure

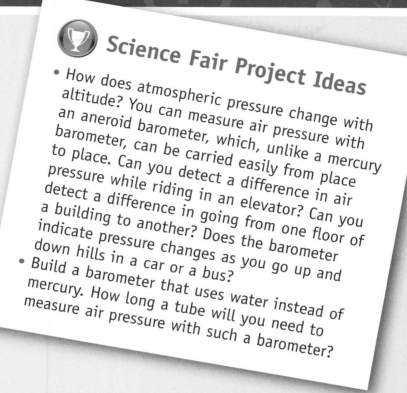

Science Fair Project Ideas

- How does atmospheric pressure change with altitude? You can measure air pressure with an aneroid barometer, which, unlike a mercury barometer, can be carried easily from place to place. Can you detect a difference in air pressure while riding in an elevator? Can you detect a difference in going from one floor of a building to another? Does the barometer indicate pressure changes as you go up and down hills in a car or a bus?

- Build a barometer that uses water instead of mercury. How long a tube will you need to measure air pressure with such a barometer?

Materials:

-an adult

-soap and warm water

-empty 1-gallon metal can with a screw-on cap (such as one used to hold paint thinner, olive oil, or maple syrup)

-cup of water

-hot plate or stove

-work gloves or pot holder

-heat-proof mat or thick stack of newspapers

-large cloth

-cold water

Because this activity requires heat and hot objects, ask an adult **to help you.**

Use soap and warm water to thoroughly wash an empty one-gallon metal can. The washing should remove any small amount of solvent, such as alcohol, that may remain in or on the can. Then pour a cup of water into the can. Leave the opening at the top of the can uncovered. **Ask an adult** to place the can on a hot plate or stove burner. If this is being done before an audience, you can do some other science magic while the water is heating.

After the water reaches the boiling point (100°C or 212°F), let it boil for several minutes so that steam replaces most of the air in the can. **Ask the adult to put on work gloves or use a pot holder** to remove the can from the heat. The can should be placed on a heat-proof mat or on a thick stack of newspapers. **The adult** should then immediately screw the cap back on or put a rubber stopper with no holes into the opening on the top of the can.

Cover the can with a large cloth that has been soaked in cold water. Wave your hands and say a few magic words as you wait for air pressure to do its job on the can. From the creaking sounds beneath the cloth, you will know that the can is being crushed. When the noises stop, remove the cloth to reveal the crushed can to the audience.

THE SCIENCE BEHIND THE MAGIC

As the water boiled, it produced steam. The steam forced air out through the top of the can, replacing most of the air that had filled the can before. The steam-filled can was closed before the steam could condense. As the steam condensed, the pressure inside the can decreased because liquid water takes up less space than steam. Meanwhile, the pressure of the air pushing on the outside of the can remained unchanged. Because the pressure on the outside of the can became much greater than the pressure on the inside, the can collapsed. For example, suppose the pressure inside the can fell to 3 N/cm^2 (4.4 lb/in^2), while the pressure outside remained at 10 N/cm^2 (14.6 lb/in^2). The difference in pressure between the outside and inside of the can would be 7 N/cm^2, or 10.2 lb/in^2. If the can's surface area was 1,500 cm^2 (230 in^2), the total force pushing inward on the can would have been

1,500 cm^2 × 7 N/cm^2 = 10,500 N, or 2,300 pounds (1.15 tons).

The can's collapse is certainly not mysterious when you understand the science behind it.

1.6 A Geyser

Materials:

- an adult
- large drinking glass
- cold water
- food coloring
- Pyrex glass flask (250 mL or larger); borrow, if possible, from school science department
- one-hole rubber stopper that fits the flask
- long piece of rigid plastic or glass tubing
- glycerin, petroleum jelly, or liquid soap
- heavy gloves or oven mitt
- hot plate or stove
- heat-proof pad or thick stack of newspaper

Because this activity requires heat and hot objects, ask an adult to help you.

Air pressure can crush a metal can, as you saw in the previous activity. The same air pressure can be used to fill a vessel with water.

The cold water that you will transfer by air pressure can be placed in a large drinking glass together with a drop or two of food coloring to make the liquid more visible. You will need a Pyrex glass flask (250 mL or larger) and a one-hole rubber stopper that fits the neck of the flask. You will also need a long piece of glass or rigid plastic tubing that will extend well into the flask and 10–15 cm (4–6 in) beyond its neck (see Figure 4a). Lubricate the outside of the tubing with petroleum jelly, glycerin, or liquid soap so that it will slide easily through the hole in the stopper.

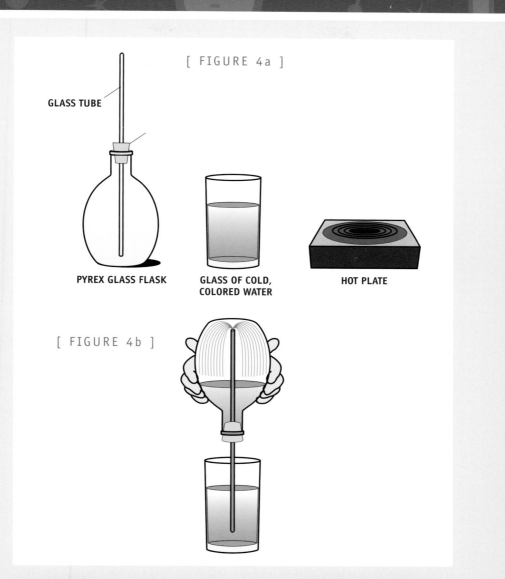

[FIGURE 4a]

GLASS TUBE

PYREX GLASS FLASK

GLASS OF COLD,
COLORED WATER

HOT PLATE

[FIGURE 4b]

4a) You will need a flask, a rubber stopper, a long piece of rigid tubing, a heat source, and a glass of cold colored water. b) Place the lower end of the glass tube extending from the inverted flask into a glass of cold water. As the steam in the flask condenses, a "geyser" will soon emerge from the tube's upper end and fill the flask.

Ask the adult to put on gloves and, using a twisting motion, carefully slide the tubing through the hole in the stopper. He or she should hold the tubing close to the stopper to avoid breaking it. If the tubing does not slide easily, get a length of tubing with a smaller diameter or find a stopper with a larger hole. **The adult should not try to force the tubing. Bad cuts can occur if the tubing breaks!**

With the equipment in place, you are now ready to carry out this part of your show **under adult supervision**. Pour about 30 mL (1 oz) of water into the Pyrex glass flask. Heat the water to boiling on a hot plate or stove burner. Let the water boil for several minutes so that the flask becomes filled with steam. (While the water is being heated, you might do another part of your act.)

After steam has replaced the air in the flask, put on heavy gloves or wear an oven mitt so that you can remove the flask from the heat. Place the flask on a heat-proof pad or a thick stack of newspapers. Immediately insert the stopper and tube into the flask, invert it, and hold it so that the lower end of the tube is in the glass of colored water, as shown in Figure 4b. Soon your audience will see a "geyser" as water flows up the tube from the glass and into the flask.

THE SCIENCE BEHIND THE MAGIC

As the steam in the flask condenses, the pressure inside the flask decreases. Air pressure forces water from the glass up the tube and into the flask. As soon as the cold water reaches the flask, the remaining steam quickly condenses, causing water to flow rapidly up the tube and into the flask, creating a geyser.

Science Fair Project Idea

In the early 1600s, Galileo heard workmen say that a pump could not lift water if the pump was more than 10 m (33 ft) above the water level. Through experiments, Galileo found that the workmen were right. Why can't pumps lift water if they are more than 10 m above the water level? Water in deep wells is often more than 30 m (100 ft) below the ground. How is water obtained from such wells?

Materials:
- Ping-Pong ball
- vacuum cleaner with hose connected to blower outlet
- funnel
- 2 balloons
- string
- support for balloons

Your audience will enjoy it when you place a Ping-Pong ball in the upwardly directed airstream from a vacuum cleaner hose connected to the blower outlet. The ball floats serenely in the airstream, as shown in Figure 5a.

After you grab the Ping-Pong ball and place it on the floor, they will marvel again as you hold a funnel firmly in the end of the vacuum cleaner hose and lift the ball from the floor. The ball darts about the inside surface of the funnel, as shown in Figure 5b, until you turn off the power to the vacuum cleaner. If you have good lung power, you can lift the ball by blowing air into the funnel.

Finally, as the grand finale to this act, you can forcibly blow air between two balloons suspended by strings from a support (Figure 5c), such as a kitchen cabinet. As if driven by some mysterious force, the balloons will move together.

THE SCIENCE BEHIND THE MAGIC

All the action in this activity is based on Bernoulli's principle. Where the velocity of a fluid (a gas or a liquid) is high, the sideways pressure is low. The Ping-Pong ball in both cases was in a fast-moving airstream. The pressure within that stream was lower than the pressure of the nonmoving air that surrounded it. Consequently, the ball was forced to stay within the fast-moving airstream.

Defies Gravity

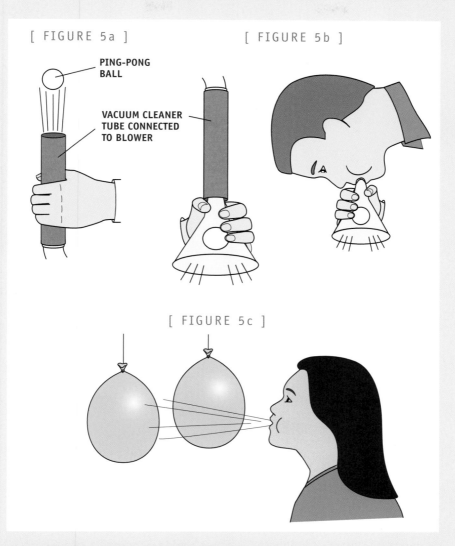

[FIGURE 5a]

PING-PONG BALL

VACUUM CLEANER TUBE CONNECTED TO BLOWER

[FIGURE 5b]

[FIGURE 5c]

5a) A Ping-Pong ball will "float" in an airstream produced by a vacuum cleaner that will blow air. b) The same airstream can be used to lift a Ping-Pong ball with an inverted funnel. If you have good lung power, you can do the same thing by blowing into the funnel. c) What happens when you blow air between two suspended balloons?

When you blew between the two balloons, the pressure between the balloons became less than the air pressure on the outside of each balloon. As a result, the balloons were forced together.

Science Fair Project Idea

You can make water defy gravity, too. Fill or partially fill a plastic medicine cup or vial with water. Place a card on the cup or vial. Hold the card in place as you turn the cup or vial upside down over a sink (at least until you are confident the water will defy gravity). Remove your hand from the card. The water will remain in the cup or vial. Of course, gravity cannot be made to disappear and it cannot really be defied. How then can you explain the fact that the water remains in the container?

1.8 A Voice-Controlled Submarine

Materials:

- eyedropper
- widemouthed bottle
- rubber stopper or large cork to fit mouth of bottle
- water

Show your audience a model for a submarine. The model consists of an eyedropper partially filled with water in a widemouthed bottle capped with a rubber stopper or large cork, as shown in Figure 6. You say, "Deep dive," and the "submarine" sinks to the bottom of the bottle. You then say, "Surface," and the vessel rises to the top of the bottle. "Submerge!" you shout, and the sub drops to a point between the surface and the bottom.

To prepare your model submarine, nearly fill the bottle with water. Draw enough water into the eyedropper so that it floats in the bottle with just the tip of the rubber bulb above the surface. Place the stopper or cork loosely into the mouth of the bottle. To make the eyedropper fall to the bottom of the bottle, push the stopper farther down into the mouth of the bottle. To make it rise, pull the stopper back up so that it just rests in the mouth of the bottle. Pushing the stopper partway into the bottle's mouth will enable you to make the eyedropper sink below the surface, but not to the bottom.

THE SCIENCE BEHIND THE MAGIC

When you push down on the stopper, you decrease the space above the water, increasing the air pressure. This increased air pressure is transferred to the water, forcing more liquid into the eyedropper. The rise of water in the eyedropper adds to its density and causes it to sink. Releasing the pressure by raising the stopper reduces the water in the eyedropper, allowing it to rise. By carefully adjusting the pressure with the stopper, you can give the eyedropper a density equal to that of the water, causing it to float in the middle of the bottle.

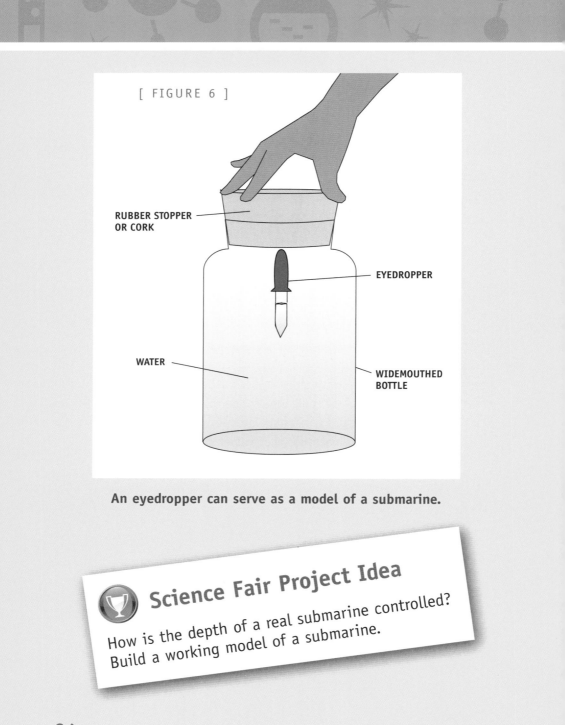

[FIGURE 6]

RUBBER STOPPER
OR CORK

EYEDROPPER

WATER

WIDEMOUTHED
BOTTLE

An eyedropper can serve as a model of a submarine.

🏆 **Science Fair Project Idea**

How is the depth of a real submarine controlled?
Build a working model of a submarine.

Chapter 2

Magic Through Chemistry

THE ACTIVITIES IN THIS CHAPTER provide observations that seem magical to those who are not familiar with chemistry. They offer no surprises to chemists.

Most of the chemicals needed to perform chemical "magic" can be found in your kitchen or bathroom. A few of the substances you will need can be purchased at a pharmacy or are probably among your school's supply of science materials. You will have to ask a science teacher if you may use those chemicals.

2.1 Dancing Raisins

Materials:
- an adult
- raisins
- small paring knife
- cutting board
- glass
- bottle of ginger ale, club soda, or seltzer water

To prepare for this scene, you will need to use a small paring knife to cut several raisins into quarters. **Ask an adult** to help you.

With the quartered raisins nearby, nearly fill a glass from a fresh bottle of ginger ale, club soda, or seltzer water. Add the raisins and instruct them to dance for your audience.

At first, the raisins will sink to the bottom of the glass. Then, they will rise to the surface, twist and turn a few times, and then sink back to the bottom of the liquid, before they rise again for another dance.

THE SCIENCE BEHIND THE MAGIC

Because raisins are denser than the beverage, they sink when you drop them into the liquid. However, gases are less soluble in water at low pressure than at the higher pressure that existed when the carbonated beverage was bottled. As a result, bubbles of carbon dioxide emerge in fizzy fashion from the solution when the bottle is opened. The bubbles of gas adhere to the raisins. As the bubbles accumulate, the total density of the raisins and adhering gas becomes less than that of the liquid, and the raisins rise to the surface. There, bumped about by rising bubbles of gas, some of the gas bubbles are knocked off the surface of the raisins, and they fall back to the bottom of the glass.

Science Fair Project Idea

Design a way to have buttons do a similar dance, using water, baking soda, and vinegar. Explain the source of the bubbles that cause the buttons to dance.

Materials:
-black ink
-2 narrow-mouthed bottles
-hot and cold water
-paper towel
-sink

This scene should be prepared immediately before the show. Fill one of two narrow-mouthed bottles to the very top with hot tap water and enough black ink to make the water very dark. The second narrow-mouthed bottle should be filled to the very top with clear, cold tap water.

Tell the audience that a genie resides in the dark-colored bottle and that you are going to try to coax her to emerge. Place a small piece of paper towel on the top of the bottle of clear, cold water. Turn it upside down and place it on top of the bottle with the hot, dark liquid, as shown in Figure 7a. The water does not fall out of the inverted bottle because the paper towel, held in place by air pressure, holds the water in the bottle. Air pressure can support a column of water 10 m high as long as there is no air above the column (see Chapter 1).

Carefully pull the piece of paper towel from between the two bottles as you utter a few words of encouragement to the genie. A "genie" will emerge from the lower bottle and move into the upper bottle, as shown in Figure 7b.

After the show, hold the bottles together as you carry them to a sink where they can be separated and emptied.

THE SCIENCE BEHIND THE MAGIC

The "genie" is the inky hot water. Because hot water is less dense than cold water, it rises slowly above the cold water as the cold water sinks below the hot water.

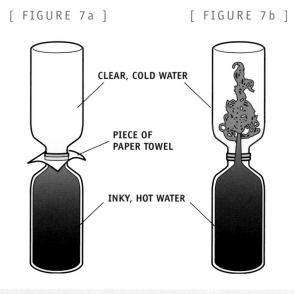

[FIGURE 7a]   [FIGURE 7b]

CLEAR, COLD WATER

PIECE OF
PAPER TOWEL

INKY, HOT WATER

7a) A bottle of cold water is covered with a piece of paper towel. The bottle is then turned upside down and placed on a bottle of hot inky water. b) When the piece of towel is removed, a "genie" emerges from the lower bottle.

Science Fair Project Ideas

- Investigate the relationship between the density of water and its temperature. Is this relationship unique to water?
- Investigate what causes the water in lakes and ponds to "turn over" in many parts of the world during late autumn and early spring.

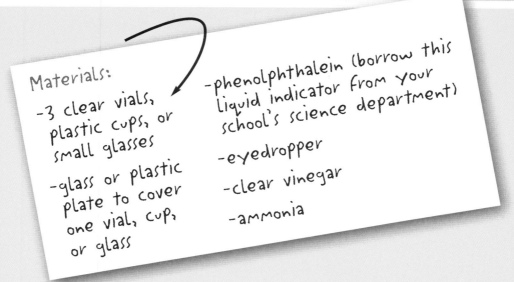

Materials:

-3 clear vials, plastic cups, or small glasses

-glass or plastic plate to cover one vial, cup, or glass

-phenolphthalein (borrow this liquid indicator from your school's science department)

-eyedropper

-clear vinegar

-ammonia

Warning: Do not put anything containing ammonia near or in your mouth or eyes!

Tell your audience you will change water to dragon's blood and then convert it back to water. Remove the cover from what appears to be an empty vial, mutter a few magic words, and proceed to pour a clear liquid into it. The clear liquid suddenly turns deep red. Pour the "dragon's blood" into another apparently empty vial and it suddenly turns clear again.

The clear liquid is water to which you previously added 10 drops of phenolphthalein and 1 drop of clear vinegar. The first "empty" cup actually contains 3 drops of ammonia. (The cover prevents the ammonia from evaporating.) The second "empty" vial contains 10 drops of vinegar.

THE SCIENCE BEHIND THE MAGIC

Phenolphthalein is an acid-base indicator. It is clear in an acid and red in a base. The drop of vinegar in the water with the 10 drops of phenolphthalein makes the water slightly acidic. Consequently, the liquid will be clear. When it is added to the vial with 3 drops of ammonia, the ammonia, which is basic, causes the phenolphthalein to turn red, making it appear to be dragon's blood.

The "dragon's blood" is then poured into the next vial, which contains 10 drops of vinegar. There is enough acidic vinegar to neutralize the ammonia and provide an excess of acid. The resulting solution is clear because phenolphthalein is clear in an acid.

2.4 Magical Bubbles

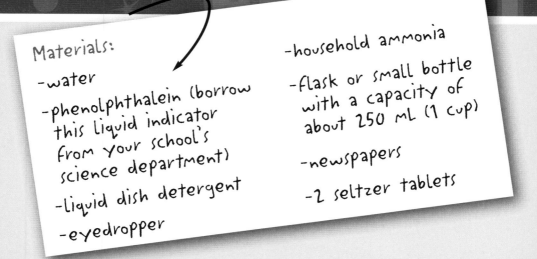

Materials:
- water
- phenolphthalein (borrow this liquid indicator from your school's science department)
- liquid dish detergent
- eyedropper
- household ammonia
- flask or small bottle with a capacity of about 250 mL (1 cup)
- newspapers
- 2 seltzer tablets

Warning: Do not put anything containing ammonia near or in your mouth or eyes!

Before the show, add about 50 mL (1.6 oz) of water, 10 drops of phenolphthalein, a squirt of liquid dish detergent, and 5 drops of household ammonia to a flask or bottle that holds about 250 mL (1 cup). The solution will be red. Place the flask on a thick stack of newspapers to protect any surface beneath the flask.

Tell your audience that when you add the magic tablets to the flask, the liquid will lose its color and a cascade of bubbles will emerge from the flask. Then drop the seltzer tablets into the flask and the bubbles that form will do the rest.

THE SCIENCE BEHIND THE MAGIC

The seltzer tablets contain sodium bicarbonate ($NaHCO_3$) and citric acid ($C_6H_8O_7$). In water, these substances react to form carbon dioxide gas. The citric acid and carbon dioxide, which form carbonic acid (H_2CO_3) in water, neutralize the ammonia and provide an excess of acid. Since phenolphthalein is clear in acid, the solution quickly loses its red color. Bubbles form and emerge from the flask as the soapy water is filled with carbon dioxide gas.

Materials:
- graduated cylinder or measuring cup
- unsweetened red grape juice
- water
- 3 glasses, plastic cups, or beakers
- eyedropper
- household ammonia
- clear vinegar

Warning: Do not put anything containing ammonia near or in your mouth or eyes!

To prepare for this scene, add 15 mL (0.5 oz) of *unsweetened* grape juice to 135 mL (4.5 oz) of water in a glass, plastic cup, or beaker. This will reduce the intense red color of the grape juice. Use an eyedropper to add about 5 drops of household ammonia to a second glass. In a third glass, place about 10 drops of vinegar. (You will need to practice to get the right amounts of ammonia and vinegar.)

Announce to your audience that you are preparing Ali Baba's magic liquid, which changes magically from red to green. Then utter a few magical words as you pour the grape juice into the second glass. To the amazement of your audience, the juice will suddenly turn green.

Then tell them that you can change the green liquid back to red. When you pour the green juice into the third glass, it will mysteriously change back to red.

Remember: Do not drink or taste any liquids used in experiments.

THE SCIENCE BEHIND THE MAGIC

Grape juice is an acid-base indicator. It turns green in a basic solution, and ammonia, as you know, is a base. Grape juice is bluish-purple in an acid. Consequently, it turns back to its original color when it is poured into the acidic vinegar.

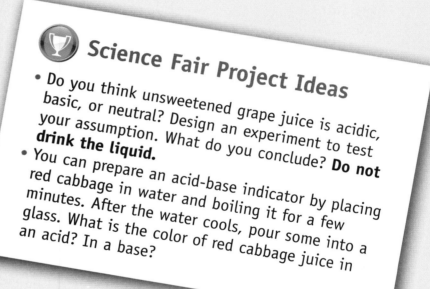

Science Fair Project Ideas

- Do you think unsweetened grape juice is acidic, basic, or neutral? Design an experiment to test your assumption. What do you conclude? **Do not drink the liquid.**
- You can prepare an acid-base indicator by placing red cabbage in water and boiling it for a few minutes. After the water cools, pour some into a glass. What is the color of red cabbage juice in an acid? In a base?

Materials:

- about 50 g (1.75 oz) of copper sulfate (buy at hardware store or ask your teacher)

- distilled water, rainwater, or soft water

- glass, plastic cup, or beaker

- stirring rod or coffee stirrer

- steel nail

- steel wool

This scene takes a few minutes because the reaction goes slowly. It can be used as an "opener" to which you return after doing several other scenes.

Before starting this bit of chemical magic, you will need to prepare a saturated solution of copper sulfate. You can do this by adding about 50 g (1.75 oz) of the blue crystals of copper sulfate to about 100 mL (3.3 oz) of distilled water, rainwater, or soft water in a glass, plastic cup, or beaker. Stir until most of the blue crystals dissolve. If necessary, add more crystals until no more will dissolve. Any excess copper sulfate can be left on the bottom of the container. You will also need a steel nail a little taller than the container that holds the blue solution of copper sulfate. Using steel wool, polish the nail to make it bright and shiny.

You might begin the scene by announcing that although alchemists never found a way to change lead into gold, you have the magical key needed to change iron into copper. After making your statement, say a few magic words as you place the steel nail into the copper sulfate solution. Mention that this is slow-acting magic, so you are going to set the vessel aside and return to it later.

When you return to the nail after a few minutes, remove the nail and show your audience that copper has formed on the part of the nail that was immersed in the liquid.

THE SCIENCE BEHIND THE MAGIC

When iron (its symbol is Fe) is placed in contact with copper ions (Cu^{+2}), which are the positive ions in copper sulfate (the negative ions are the sulfate ions, SO_4^{-2}), the iron atoms lose electrons to the copper ions. We say the iron is oxidized by the copper ions. As a result, iron ions (Fe^{+2}) dissolve in the solution, and copper ions, having gained electrons, are deposited as copper atoms (Cu^0) on the iron nail. The reaction is summarized by the equations below. (A zero above and to the right of the symbol for an atom means the atom has no charge; it has not been ionized.)

$$Fe^0 \longrightarrow Fe^{+2} + 2 \text{ electrons}$$
$$Cu^{+2} + 2 \text{ electrons} \longrightarrow Cu^0$$

The net reaction—the sum of the two reactions—is

$$Fe^0 + Cu^{+2} \longrightarrow Fe^{+2} + Cu^0.$$

Science Fair Project Idea

Investigate the following questions and write a report: What is alchemy? Who were the alchemists? What did they do? What was the philosopher's stone?

2.7 Turning Aladdin's Lamp Oil Into Ink

Materials:

- teaspoon
- cornstarch or flour
- 2 glasses, beakers, or plastic cups
- water
- tincture of iodine

To prepare for this act, add about 1/4 teaspoon of cornstarch or flour to an empty glass, beaker, or plastic cup. In an identical container about 2/3 full of water, add about 1/4 teaspoon of tincture of iodine and stir to form a straw-colored liquid. Iodine is poisonous, so keep it away from your eyes and mouth. Be sure to wash the glasses and spoon thoroughly with soap and water after the show!

As the scene begins, point to the straw-colored liquid and tell your audience that you are going to change Aladdin's lamp oil to ink. Then pour the straw-colored liquid into the vessel that holds the "magic powder" (cornstarch). After you pour the liquid back and forth from one container to the other several times, the liquid will turn dark blue.

THE SCIENCE BEHIND THE MAGIC

Starch and iodine combine to form a dark blue compound. In fact, the formation of a dark blue color when iodine is added serves as a test for starch. Similarly, if a dark blue color appears when starch is added to an unknown liquid, that liquid must contain iodine.

Science Fair Project Idea

Do some research to find out how iodine can be used to test for the starch found in foods such as potatoes and bread. Then use your knowledge to make predictions about the presence of starch in a variety of foods. Test your predictions under adult supervision.

🏆 2.8 Written Secrets

Materials:

- an adult
- pieces of paper about 10 cm × 10 cm (4 in × 4 in)
- water
- hard surface, such as a kitchen counter
- ballpoint pen
- pan
- lemon juice
- toothpicks
- sugar
- teaspoon
- medicine cup
- warm water
- kitchen clamps
- stove or hot plate
- pail of water
- cobalt chloride ($CoCl_2 \bullet 6H_2O$) (ask to borrow from school science department)
- graduated cylinder or measuring cup
- small artist's brush
- salt
- drinking glass
- soft pencil

One or all of the scenes in this act can be used to reveal to an audience invisible messages left by a "spirit," "witch," or other medium of your choice.

A HARD-PRESSED MESSAGE (for a small audience)

A mechanical form of invisible writing can be prepared in a way similar to that used to place watermarks on writing paper. Dip a piece of paper in water. Put the wet paper on a hard surface, such as a kitchen counter.

Place a piece of dry paper on the wet paper. Using a ballpoint pen, press down hard as you write a message. It could be a warm greeting, such as a smiley face or WELCOME TO THE SHOW; it could also be a foreboding message, such as BEWARE OF MAGIC-MAKING SCIENTISTS!

Set the wet paper aside to dry. When it has dried, the writing will not be apparent. Dip the paper in water and hold it up to the light. The letters or marks that make up the message will transmit light better than the rest of the paper. Consequently, the message will be quite visible as you look through it, facing a bright window or light.

If you like, this could be used as an opening scene. Each person in the audience could be given one hard-pressed message. They could then dip the paper in a pail of water and hold it up to the light.

CHEMICAL MESSAGES

Because these activities require a stove or hot plate and the possibility of flames, ask an adult for help. Keep a pan of water nearby. Should a piece of paper begin to burn, put it in the water.

A commonly used invisible ink is lemon juice. Use the wide end of a toothpick dipped in lemon juice to write a message on a small piece of paper. Keep dipping the toothpick into the lemon juice as you write. There should be a continuous film of lemon juice along each letter you write. After you have finished writing the message, set the paper aside and let the "ink" dry.

While the lemon juice is drying, write another message on another small piece of paper, using saliva (something you always have with you) as the ink and another toothpick as your pen.

Write a third invisible message, using a toothpick and a saturated solution of sugar. Add a teaspoonful of sugar to a medicine cup. Nearly fill the cup with warm water and stir with the toothpick you will use to write the message.

When the "ink" on all your messages has dried, you will be ready to reveal the hidden messages. **Under adult supervision**, use a pair of kitchen clamps to hold each piece of paper, in turn, over a stove burner or hot plate, as shown in Figure 8. Hold the paper well above the hot surface so that the paper does not burn. **A pail of water should be beside the stove in case the paper does begin to burn.**

Slowly, the message written in invisible ink on each piece of paper will appear, and you can then show it to your audience.

A CHEMICAL MESSAGE IN BLUE

To write this invisible message, you will need to prepare a solution of cobalt chloride ($CoCl_2 \bullet 6H_2O$). Dissolve as much cobalt chloride as possible in 25 mL (1 oz) of water. This saturated solution will serve as your ink. Use a small artist's brush to write a message on a small piece of paper.

When the water in the solution has evaporated, the tiny, nearly invisible pink crystals of cobalt chloride will remain. **Under adult supervision**, use a pair of kitchen clamps to hold the paper over a stove burner or hot plate, as shown in Figure 8. Hold the paper well above the hot surface so that the paper does not burn. **Keep a pail of water beside the stove in case the paper does begin to burn.**

The message you wrote on the paper will appear in blue "ink."

A SALTY HIDDEN MESSAGE

Prepare a small amount of salt solution using salt and warm water. Dissolve as much salt as you can. Dip the broad end of a toothpick into the salt solution and use it as a pen to write a message on a sheet of paper. Dip your "pen" into the salty "ink" often to be sure plenty of salt gets onto the paper.

After the liquid has thoroughly dried, the message remains invisible. To read what was written, you can gently rub the paper with the side of the soft graphite in a pencil. Rub in different directions. You will hear a scratchy sound when you are moving the pencil over the salt, and the letters will appear.

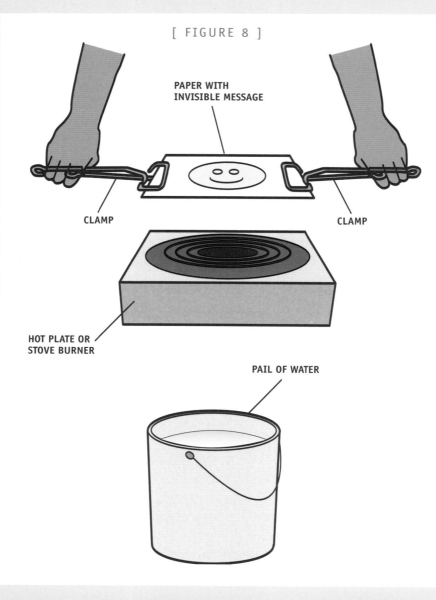

[FIGURE 8]

PAPER WITH
INVISIBLE MESSAGE

CLAMP

CLAMP

HOT PLATE OR
STOVE BURNER

PAIL OF WATER

The secret message written in invisible ink can be revealed if the
paper on which the message is written is carefully heated.

THE SCIENCE BEHIND THE MAGIC

When you wrote the hard-pressed message, you squeezed and flattened the wood fibers in the paper. This made the paper thinner. As a result, it transmitted more light than the thicker paper surrounding the message.

The "inks" used in the chemical messages all contained organic compounds (compounds that contain carbon). When these organic substances were heated, they decomposed, leaving primarily carbon, which is a black element.

The chemical message in blue appears because the water in the hydrated *pink* crystals was removed when the paper was heated. What remained on the paper were the clearly visible blue crystals of anhydrous (without water) cobalt chloride ($CoCl_2$).

With time, the blue crystals will react with moisture in the air and re-form pink hydrated crystals.

Sodium chloride ($NaCl$), which is ordinary table salt, is not an organic compound (it has no carbon). Consequently, heating dried salt would not produce a visible message. However, when you rub the soft graphite pencil over the letters you have written in saltwater, the graphite adheres to the paper but not to the $NaCl$. The message you wrote appears white on the dark (graphite) background.

Science Fair Project Idea

Develop invisible inks of your own and use them to write secret messages.

Materials:
- an adult
- matches
- candle
- candleholder
- lamp chimney, or glass or plastic cylinder
- wood blocks

Because you will be using matches and working with a burning candle, do this trick under adult supervision.

Light a candle and let it burn for several minutes. Then blow out the candle. You will notice that a stream of light-colored smoke continues to rise from the wick. If you bring a lighted match to that stream of smoke several centimeters above the wick, the flame will follow the smoke stream downward and reignite the wick.

For an audience, this trick is best done with a clear lamp chimney or a glass or plastic cylinder over the candle, as shown in Figure 9. The top of the cylinder should be about 10 cm (4 in) above the wick to make the distance that the flame jumps more dramatic. The bottom should be placed on wood blocks.

When you begin the scene, the candle is burning. You announce that you will blow out the candle and relight it without bringing a match to the wick. You then light a match, blow out the candle, and bring the match to the top of the chimney, where it can ignite the smoke streaming from the wick. The flame will follow the smoke back to the wick. You can repeat this several times, but the candle must burn long enough to produce a good stream of wax vapor after the flame is blown out.

THE SCIENCE BEHIND THE MAGIC

When you light a candle, the wick burns and melts some of the wax at the top of the candle. The liquid wax moves up the wick by capillary action. As the wax reaches the flame, it changes to a gas and burns.

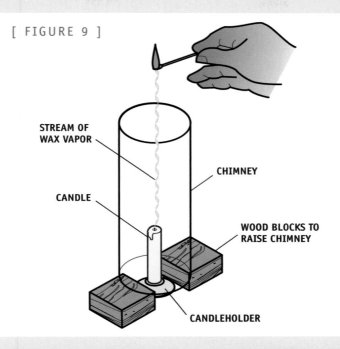

[FIGURE 9]

STREAM OF
WAX VAPOR

CHIMNEY

CANDLE

WOOD BLOCKS TO
RAISE CHIMNEY

CANDLEHOLDER

A stream of wax vapor rising from a just-extinguished candle is flammable. If ignited, the flame will follow the vapor trail back to the wick and relight the candle. Blocks are placed under the chimney so that air can flow under it and provide a good source of oxygen for the burning candle.

When you blow out a candle, a stream of flammable wax vapor rises from the wick. Bringing a match to the vapor ignites it, and the flame follows the vapor trail down to its origin. Once the wick cools and fails to emit any more vapor, you cannot reignite it from afar.

Science Fair Project Idea

What is capillary action? Investigate how it works. Design an experiment to demonstrate capillary action at work.

2.10 A Blue Bottle

Materials:
- an adult
- safety glasses
- plastic or latex gloves
- 500 ml glass flask, preferably round with a flat base
- rubber stopper that fits flask
- 400 ml of water
- balance with weighing papers
- Potassium hydroxide (KOH) (ask to borrow from school science department)
- spatula or spoon to transfer chemicals
- dextrose (glucose) (ask to borrow from school science department or buy from pharmacy)
- methylene blue (ask to borrow from school science department)

Because toxic chemicals are used in this activity, prepare the solution under adult supervision. Wear safety glasses while working with these chemicals.

If you can obtain the necessary chemicals and glass flask from your school's science department, this scene could provide a dramatic start and conclusion to your science-through-magic program.

Pointing to a glass flask that holds a cloudy liquid, you say, "That's strange; this liquid used to be blue." You then shake the flask, keeping your hand firmly over the rubber stopper in its neck. The fluid in the bottle suddenly turns blue.

The blue color will slowly fade with time. It will return each time you shake it. If you start your program with this scene, you can return to it periodically throughout the show and conclude with it.

Put on a pair of plastic or latex gloves. The solution is prepared by adding approximately 2.0 grams (0.07 oz) of potassium hydroxide (KOH) to about 400 mL of water. **(Potassium hydroxide is a poisonous solid similar to lye. Keep it away from your skin, eyes, and mouth.)** Use a spatula or spoon to transfer the potassium hydroxide from its bottle to a weighing paper on the balance. Once weighed, the solid can be poured from the paper into the flask.

Heat will be produced when this strong base is added to water. After the solution cools, add 1.2 grams (0.04 oz) of dextrose (glucose) and a pinch of methylene blue. Stir to dissolve the two solids.

The solution is not stable, so you should prepare a fresh solution before each show.

THE SCIENCE BEHIND THE MAGIC

In a basic solution, methylene blue turns to a cloudy gray compound. However, when the solution is mixed with oxygen in the air, the cloudy compound is oxidized back to methylene blue, so the solution becomes blue again. In fact, if you look closely, you will see that the surface of the cloudy gray compound, which is in contact with air, remains blue.

Materials:
- an adult
- eyedropper
- black ink
- water
- drinking glass
- liquid bleach
- spoon
- facial tissue
- felt-tip pen
- ballpoint pen

Liquid bleach is poisonous. Keep it away from your eyes, nose, and mouth. Wash your hands thoroughly after you finish blotting away the message.

Bleaches contain a chemical that will react with many colored substances to form colorless substances. Can bleach make a dark, inky solution turn clear? Can it make a message written in normal visible ink disappear?

Add a drop or two of black ink to some water in a glass and stir to mix. **Under adult supervision**, add a few drops of liquid bleach to the dark mixture. Stir for a minute or two, and the liquid will turn clear if you have added enough bleach.

How many drops of bleach are required to clear up one drop of ink in water?

Can the same bleach on a facial tissue be used to blot away a letter written with a felt-tip pen? Can it be used to blot away a letter written with a ballpoint pen?

A prediction: See if you can predict how many drops of bleach will be needed to clear up two drops of ink in water.

Were you right?

Can you predict how many drops will be needed to clear up three drops of ink in water? To clear up four drops of ink?

2.12 Disappearing Glass

Materials:
- plain, clear drinking glass or plastic cylinder
- water
- pencil
- coin
- teacup
- Pyrex glass tubing
- cooking oil

When light passes from air to water, glass, diamond, or any other transparent material, it bends. You can see this for yourself. Fill a plain, clear drinking glass or plastic cylinder with water. Put a pencil into the glass and look at the pencil from the side. You will see that the pencil appears to be broken at the point where it enters the water. Light passing from the pencil through the water bends when it enters the air.

Another way to see this effect is to place a coin on the bottom of an empty teacup, as shown in Figure 10. Lower your head so that the coin just disappears from your view. Ask someone to slowly pour water into the cup. The coin will become visible again.

If two substances bend light coming from air through the same angle, one of the substances will become invisible if placed in the other. Because the two substances behave in the same way with respect to light, light passing from one to the other will not be bent or reflected. Therefore, if one object is placed inside the other, light goes right through the one inside without being affected in any way.

Cooking oil and Pyrex glass bend light coming from air through the same angle. Consequently, Pyrex glass will disappear if placed in cooking oil. If possible, borrow a few short lengths of Pyrex glass tubing from your school. Place the short lengths of tubing in a clear glass of cooking oil. You will see the tubing slowly disappear as the air in the tubes becomes filled with cooking oil.

[FIGURE 10]

Lower your head so that the coin just disappears from view. The coin will become visible again when water is slowly poured into the cup.

Chapter 3

Toys You Can Make

IN CHAPTERS 1 AND 2, you learned about scientific principles of air and chemistry by doing magic tricks. Maybe it is more surprising to you that toys can also provide you with an understanding of science. This chapter is filled with projects that use toys as the basis for experiments.

In colonial America, most of the toys that children played with were homemade. Often, they were made by the children. You may or may not have ever made your own toy. In this chapter, you will have a chance to make some toys. The toys can be used to carry out a number of experiments that will help you to learn more about science. Perhaps by the time you finish this chapter, you will want to make some toys of your own design. If you do, can you use any of them for experiments?

Materials:

- hammer
- large nail
- empty 39-oz metal coffee can and plastic cover
- ruler
- marking pen
- scissors
- rubber band about 18 cm (7 in) long and 0.3 cm (1/8 in) wide
- a friend
- twist tie
- a weight, such as a fishing sinker or heavy washers— about 60 g (2 oz)
- long, smooth, level surface

You can make a toy that will roll back to you after you give it a push that causes it to roll away from you along a smooth, level surface. To begin, use a hammer and a large nail to make two holes in the bottom of a 39-oz coffee can. The holes should be placed along the diameter of the bottom of the can. Each of the holes should be 1.9 cm (3/4 in) from the center of the diameter, but on opposite sides of the center, as shown in Figure 11a.

Make a similar pair of holes in the can's plastic snap-on cover. You can make these holes by simply pushing the nail through the plastic. Next, use scissors to cut open a rubber band that is about 18 cm (7 in) long and 0.3 cm (1/8 in) wide. Thread the ends of the rubber band through the holes in the bottom and top of the can and tie the ends together over the top of the can, as shown in Figure 11b. Finally, have a friend hold the can and pull the plastic top away from the opening so that you can reach the rubber band inside the can. Be careful if the coffee can opening is sharp, because the metal can cut you. Use a twist tie to fasten a weight, such as a fishing sinker or some heavy washers, to

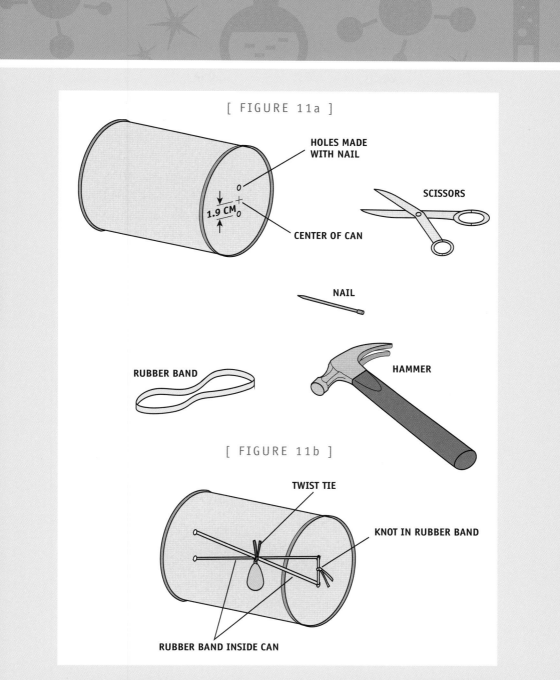

[FIGURE 11a]

HOLES MADE
WITH NAIL

SCISSORS

CENTER OF CAN

1.9 CM

NAIL

RUBBER BAND

HAMMER

[FIGURE 11b]

TWIST TIE

KNOT IN RUBBER BAND

RUBBER BAND INSIDE CAN

Use the materials shown in (a) to make the comeback toy shown in (b).

the center of both strands of the rubber band as shown. Be sure the weight is not touching the can but is suspended above the side of the can. Fasten the twist tie securely to both strands of the rubber band. The weight will keep the center of the bands from turning.

Replace the cover and place your homemade toy on its side on a smooth, level surface. Give it a push and watch it roll away from you. After a short time, it will stop and roll back to you. Can you explain why? If not, think about what is happening to the rubber band as the can rolls forward. What is happening to the weight?

Science Fair Project Idea

You can do an experiment similar to Experiment 3.1 using a rope swing. Sit on the swing and have someone give you a push so that you swing around in one direction. What happens after you stop spinning in that direction? Can you explain why? How is your motion on the swing similar to the motion of the comeback toy? Are there any differences?

Materials:

- an adult
- wooden coffee stirrers or Popsicle sticks
- 30-cm (12-in) length of 20-gauge copper wire
- 2 heavy steel washers or nuts
- full-length mirror
- drill and small bit
- straight pin
- a friend
- horizontal bar
- paper clips or short lengths of wire
- pen or pencil
- colored markers
- light cardboard
- glue
- drinking straw
- knife
- large potato

Obtain a wooden coffee stirrer or the stick from a frozen fruit bar. Can you balance the stick on the tip of your finger?

You were probably able to balance the stick by laying it horizontally on your finger. But can you balance it vertically on your finger?

You can easily balance the stick vertically if you make a balancing toy. To make such a toy, wind the center portion of a 30-cm (12-in) length of 20-gauge copper wire tightly around the stick near one end, as shown in Figure 12. Bend the wire down on each side of the stick, make small hooklike bends at the ends of the wire, and place a heavy steel washer or nut on each hook.

You will find that the stick, even when vertical, will balance on your finger.

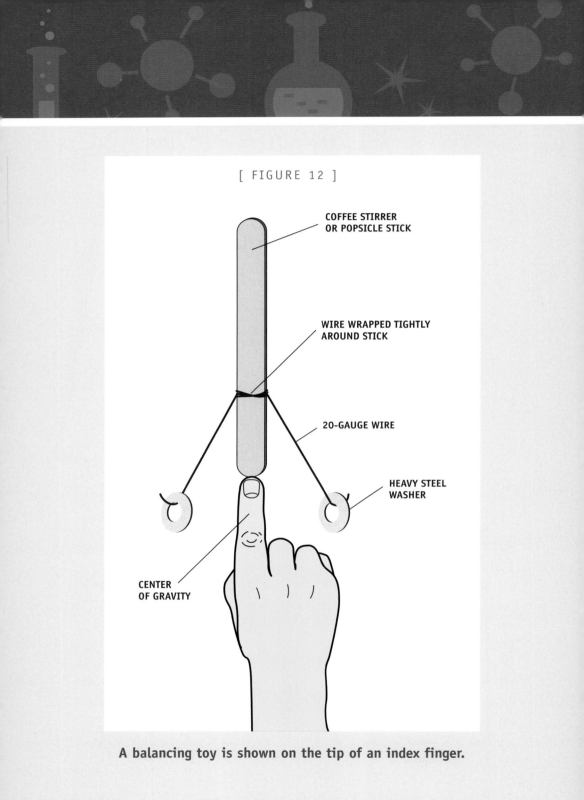

[FIGURE 12]

COFFEE STIRRER
OR POPSICLE STICK

WIRE WRAPPED TIGHTLY
AROUND STICK

20-GAUGE WIRE

HEAVY STEEL
WASHER

CENTER
OF GRAVITY

A balancing toy is shown on the tip of an index finger.

To understand why the stick will now balance in a vertical position, you need to know about its center of gravity. The center of gravity of any object is the point where all the weight of an object can be considered to be located. It is the object's balance point. When its center of gravity is supported, an object will not rotate in any direction unless pushed.

As you found, the center of gravity of the stick alone is at its center. Before attaching the washers, when you placed the center of the stick horizontally on your finger, the stick balanced. But when you placed the stick vertically on your fingertip, it fell off. To see why, consider your own center of gravity. It is close to the middle of your body, several inches below your navel. Stand on one leg in front of a full-length mirror. Notice that to maintain your balance, you must lean toward the leg on which you are standing. By so doing, you keep your center of gravity over the foot you are standing on. As a result, your body does not rotate about your center of gravity and cause you to fall. If you try to lift one leg without leaning, you will find that you begin to fall toward the leg you lifted.

Turn sideways in front of the mirror. Bend down and touch your toes as you watch your body in the mirror. You will see that as you bend, you move your rump back. By so doing, you keep your center of gravity over your feet so that your body does not rotate and cause you to fall. If both your heels are against a wall, you will find that you cannot touch your toes. Why not?

Now, think about your balancing toy. You found it was impossible to balance the stick when it was vertical. You could not keep the stick's center of gravity directly over your fingertip. But when you added equal weights to opposite sides of the stick and kept them beneath the lower end of the stick, it was easy to make it balance. By adding weights, you lowered the center of gravity until it was below your fingertip.

You can do the same thing with the stick alone. Just put its center of gravity below its point of support.

Ask an adult to drill a small hole near one end of a stick like the one you used to make your balancing toy. Put a pin through the hole. Hold on to the head of the pin. Let the stick swing on the pin. Where does the stick come to rest? Where is its center of gravity relative to its point of support?

Ask a friend to hang from a horizontal bar with both hands. The bar should be slightly higher than your friend's reach so that his or her feet are off the floor. Then ask your friend to hang by one hand instead of two. Watch what happens to your friend's center of gravity. Is it below the hand from which he or she is suspended?

Move the wire that wraps around your balance toy farther up the stick so that the weights are above your fingertip, as shown in Figure 13a. Do you think the toy will balance now? Can you explain why?

What do you think will happen if you lower the weights again but bend the wire so that the weights are to one side of the stick, as shown in Figure 13b? Were you right? Can you explain the stick's new balance position?

Do you think you can make the stick balance if you substitute paper clips or short lengths of wire for the heavy washers or nuts? Try it. Were you right? Can you explain your results?

To amuse your friends or family, build the "always-upright clown." Draw a clown on a sheet of light cardboard. Add the proper colors and glue him to a drinking straw that you have stuck in the center of half a potato, as shown in Figure 14a. No matter which way you tilt the clown, he will always return to an upright position. Can you explain why? Using common materials you can find around your house, you might like to build some of the center-of-gravity toys shown in Figure 14b.

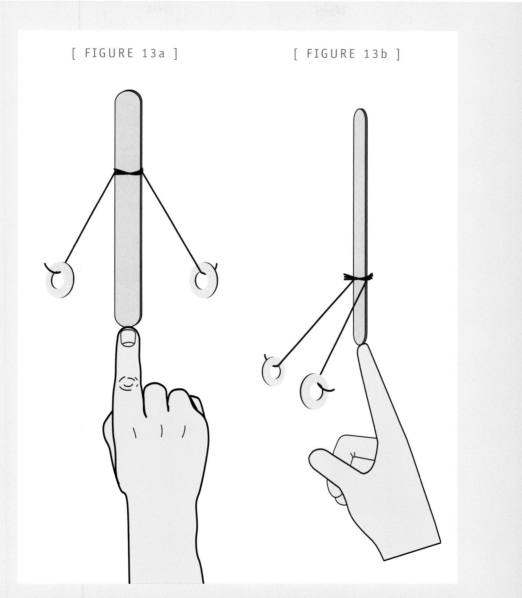

[FIGURE 13a]   [FIGURE 13b]

13a) Will your balancing toy be stable if the weights are above your fingertip? b) Will the toy balance with both weights to one side and below your fingertip? If so, how will it look when balanced?

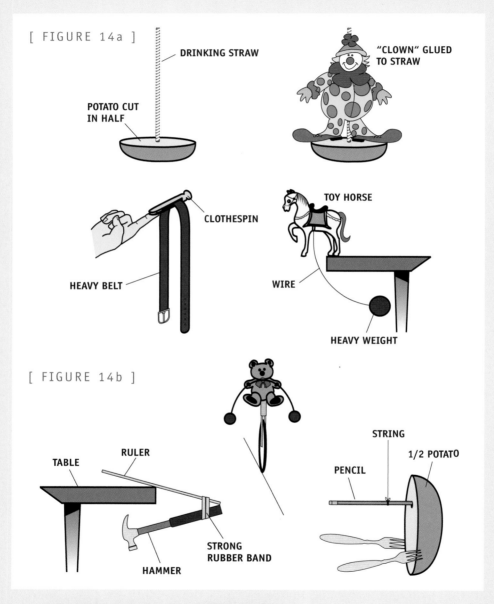

[FIGURE 14a]

DRINKING STRAW

"CLOWN" GLUED TO STRAW

POTATO CUT IN HALF

CLOTHESPIN

TOY HORSE

HEAVY BELT

WIRE

HEAVY WEIGHT

[FIGURE 14b]

STRING

1/2 POTATO

TABLE

RULER

PENCIL

STRONG RUBBER BAND

HAMMER

14a) Make an always-upright clown.
b) Some examples of balancing toys you might like to make

Science Fair Project Ideas

- Design and build some more balancing toys.
- Place the ends of a yardstick or meterstick on the index fingers of your outstretched hands. Slowly slide your hands together. At what point do they meet on the stick? Can you explain why they meet there? Now place a lump of clay near one end of the yardstick or meterstick and repeat the experiment. Where do your hands meet this time? Can you offer an explanation? Design an experiment to test your explanation.
- Investigate how the center of gravity is related to automobile safety.
- Investigate how the center of gravity is related to sports. Of special interest might be the claim that a pole vaulter's center of gravity passes under, not over, the bar.

3.3 Make a Frictionless Toy

Materials:

- an adult
- 1/4-in plywood
- empty thread spool, or cork, cork borer, and glue
- 30-cm (12-in) round balloon
- saw
- ruler
- drill and bit (1/16-in)
- sandpaper
- smooth, level surface
- thin pieces of wood or newspapers
- table that has a smooth surface, or a long, smooth board
- carpenter's level

You can build a frictionless toy air car from plywood, an empty thread spool, and a 30-cm (12-inch) round balloon. **Ask an adult** to help you build the car. You will need a square piece of 1/4-in plywood, 7.5 cm (3 in) on a side. The plywood should be smooth on both sides. If the face of the wood square is not perfectly smooth, use some sandpaper to make it so.

Ask an adult to drill a hole 1.5 mm (1/16 in) in diameter through the exact center of the wood square. An empty thread spool can then be glued to the center of the square. Alternatively, you can bore a hole through a cork and glue it to the wood square. In either case, be sure the hole through the spool or cork is in line with the hole that was drilled through the wood square (see Figure 15).

Place the air car on a very smooth, level surface, such as a kitchen or laboratory counter. (Use a carpenter's level to determine if the surface

Air Car

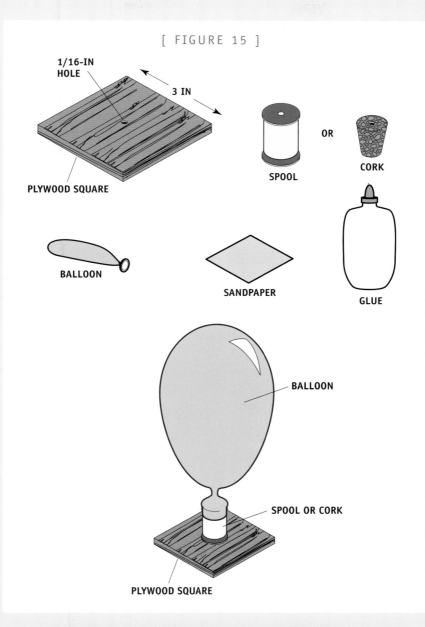

[FIGURE 15]

1/16-IN HOLE

3 IN

PLYWOOD SQUARE

SPOOL

OR

CORK

BALLOON

SANDPAPER

GLUE

BALLOON

SPOOL OR CORK

PLYWOOD SQUARE

You can make an air car that is nearly frictionless.

is level.) Blow up a balloon and attach it to the spool as shown in the drawing. Release the neck of the balloon so that air can flow through the spool and the hole in the square. The air will lift the car slightly, providing a nearly frictionless surface on which the air car can move. Give the car a gentle push. It should move at what appears to be constant speed along the smooth, level surface. If it does not, you may need to sand the lower surface of the wood again; you may need a stronger balloon to force more air through the hole; or you may need to make the hole bigger by using a slightly larger drill bit than the one you used before.

What happens to the car when all the air has left the balloon?

Fill the balloon again and give the toy air car a push along a smooth, level surface. What do you notice about the car's speed if you give it a stronger push? A weaker push?

You know that if you drop your toy car or anything else, it will fall because the earth's gravity pulls everything toward its center. Similarly, a ball placed on even a slight incline will roll because the force of gravity pulls it closer to the earth.

Your air car is an excellent gravity detector. To see this for yourself, inflate the car's balloon and place the car on an incline. To make a slight incline, put thin pieces of wood or newspapers under two legs of a level table that has a smooth surface. You can do the same thing with a long, smooth board.

What happens when you place your air car at the top of the incline and let go? Why do you think the car moves faster and faster as it slides down the incline?

What happens to the way the car moves if you make the incline steeper? If you make it less steep?

How can you use your air car to tell whether a kitchen counter, a table, or a smooth floor is level?

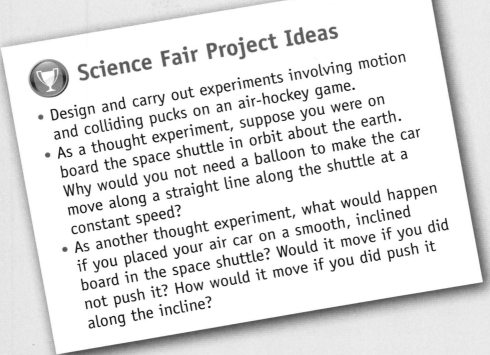

Science Fair Project Ideas

- Design and carry out experiments involving motion and colliding pucks on an air-hockey game.
- As a thought experiment, suppose you were on board the space shuttle in orbit about the earth. Why would you not need a balloon to make the car move along a straight line along the shuttle at a constant speed?
- As another thought experiment, what would happen if you placed your air car on a smooth, inclined board in the space shuttle? Would it move if you did not push it? How would it move if you did push it along the incline?

Materials:
- air car you made in previous experiment
- string
- duct tape
- smooth, level table
- washers
- paper clip

You have seen that when gravity pulls your air car down an incline, the car moves faster and faster. Gravity is one way to exert a force (pull) on the car, but you can exert a force on the car yourself. You did that when you made the car move by giving it a push. You can also exert a force on the car by pulling it. If you attach a string to the top of the plywood with a piece of duct tape, you can pull it quite easily.

Fill the balloon of your air car and attach it to the spool or cork. Then use the string to pull the car over a smooth, level surface with a small but steady force, as shown in Figure 16a. What happens to the car's speed as you pull on it?

To apply a more constant force, attach the free end of the string to a washer, as shown in Figure 16b. Let the string, supported by a bent paper clip, hang over the end of a smooth table or counter on which the car will move. Describe the motion of the car when the washer pulls on it. What is causing the steady force on the air car now?

Attach a second washer to the string so that the pull (force) on the car is twice as great. How does the motion of the car with two washers pulling it compare with its motion when one washer pulls it? How do you think the motion of two air cars hooked together with tape and pulled by two washers would compare with the motion of one car pulled by one washer?

If you used a string to pull the car in the space shuttle, would its speed increase as you pulled it? Could you use a washer hanging over a table to pull your car in the space shuttle?

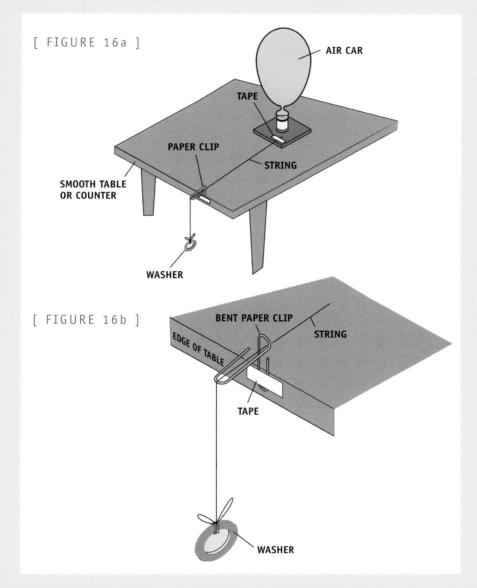

[FIGURE 16a]

AIR CAR

TAPE

PAPER CLIP

STRING

SMOOTH TABLE
OR COUNTER

WASHER

[FIGURE 16b]

BENT PAPER CLIP

STRING

EDGE OF TABLE

TAPE

WASHER

16a) What happens to the air car's speed when a constant force pulls on it? b) A close-up view of the free end of the string running through a bent paper clip

Materials:

- air car you made in Experiment 3.3
- tape
- square or disk-shaped ceramic magnets
- smooth, level table
- 2 balloons
- door frame
- string
- cloth
- plastic rulers, combs, or containers
- magnet
- long stick
- metal water pipe

Gravity and your muscles are not the only forces that can act on your air car. Magnets and electricity can push or pull it as well. Tape a small square or disk-shaped ceramic magnet to your air car, as shown in Figure 17.

Hold a second magnet close to the one on the air car. What happens? How can you tell that a force is acting? What happens to the direction of the force if you turn the magnet you are holding around?

If the two magnets are a fixed distance apart, the force will be constant. What happens to the speed of the air car when you use the magnets to exert a constant force? What happens to the strength of the magnetic force if you bring the two magnets closer together? How do you know?

How can the magnets be used as a brake to reduce the car's speed? If you keep the "brakes" on, can you make the car back up?

If you live in an area where winter brings cold weather, the air inside a building will be dry. In dry winter air, or on any day when the humidity is low, conditions are ideal for doing experiments with static electricity. Static means "stationary," so static electricity involves electrical charges that are not moving.

Static charges dissipate or leak away quickly in humid air, but in dry air you can charge many objects by simply rubbing them with cloth or paper. On such a day, blow up two identical balloons and seal them. Then use tape and strings to hang the balloons from a door frame, as shown in Figure 18. Charge both balloons by rubbing them with a cloth. Notice how the like-charged balloons repel each other. Try charging other objects such as plastic rulers, combs, and plastic containers. Do these objects all repel the balloons, or are the balloons attracted to some of them? Does the distance between charged objects have any effect on the strength of the force between them? How can you tell?

[FIGURE 17]

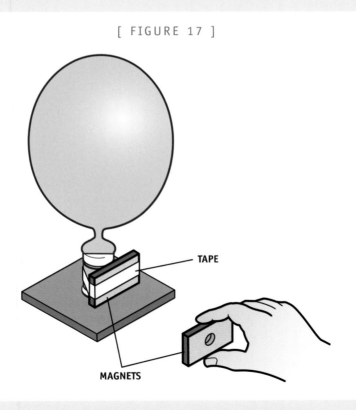

TAPE

MAGNETS

Can magnetism be used to move an air car?

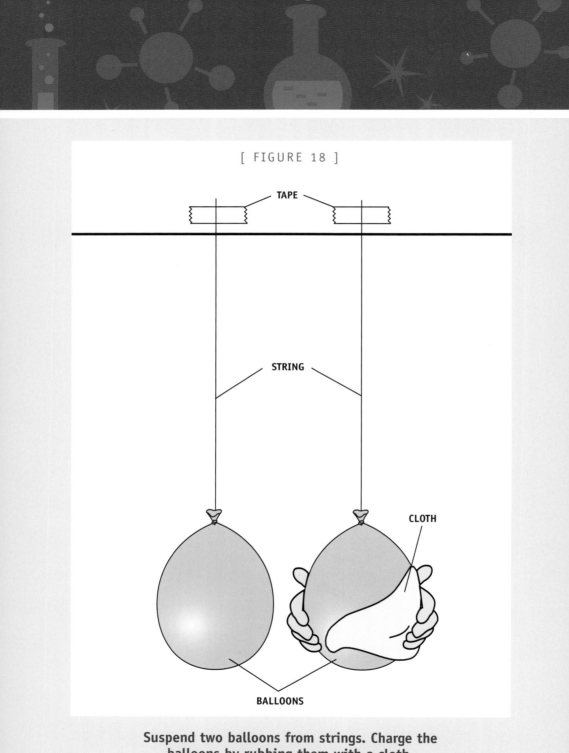

[FIGURE 18]

TAPE

STRING

CLOTH

BALLOONS

Suspend two balloons from strings. Charge the balloons by rubbing them with a cloth.

Objects that attract the balloons are said to carry a charge opposite that of the balloons. For example, if the balloons are positively charged, a charged object that attracts the balloons has a negative charge. After charging these objects, has any charge collected on your hands or clothes? How can you find out? Has a charge collected on the cloth?

Tape a magnet to a long stick. Touch the magnet to a metal water pipe to remove any charge that may be on it. Then bring the magnet near, but not touching, a charged balloon. Does the magnet exert any force on the charged balloon? What does this tell you?

From what you have learned, use static electricity to exert a force on your air car. How can you use electric charge to accelerate your car? How can you use electric charge to act as a brake on your car?

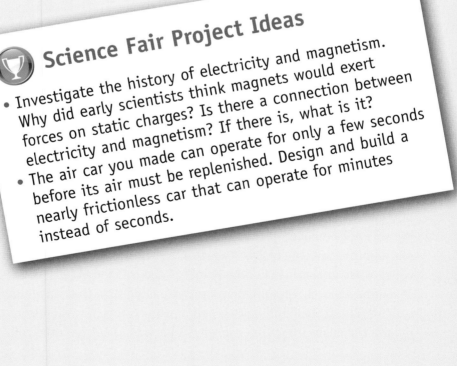

Science Fair Project Ideas

- Investigate the history of electricity and magnetism. Why did early scientists think magnets would exert forces on static charges? Is there a connection between electricity and magnetism? If there is, what is it?
- The air car you made can operate for only a few seconds before its air must be replenished. Design and build a nearly frictionless car that can operate for minutes instead of seconds.

Materials:

- 30-cm (12-in) length of 24-gauge enamel-coated copper wire
- ruler
- tape
- wire cutters
- sandpaper
- two 10-cm (4-in) pieces of bare 20-gauge copper wire (or paper clips)
- thumbtacks
- short piece of soft pine board
- 2 flat, square or round ceramic or rubberized magnets
- insulated wires with connectors
- 2 D-cells and battery holder(s)

An electric motor converts electrical energy to mechanical energy that can do work. It is basically a coil of wire, a magnet, and a battery. To make a toy electric motor, you can begin by making the coil. Wrap a 30-cm (12-in) length of 24-gauge enamel-coated copper wire four times around the width of a ruler. Remove the coil of wire from the ruler. Wrap the two free ends of the wire once around opposite sides of the coil and extend them straight out from the coil (see Figure 19a). Use two small pieces of tape to hold the coiled wires in place. The entire length of the coil and extended wires should be about 3 inches. If the wires extending from the coil are too long, snip off part of their ends with a pair of wire cutters. Use sandpaper to remove the enamel from the two wires that extend out from the coil.

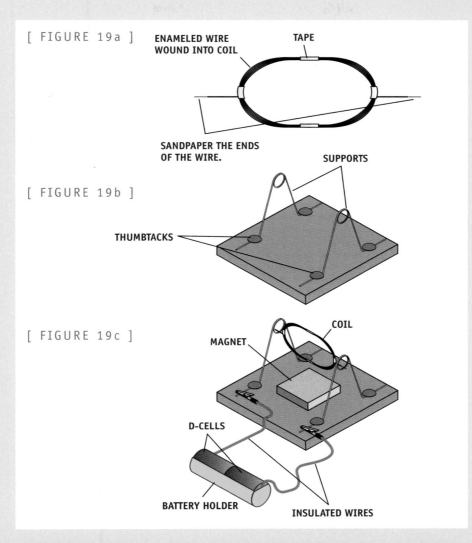

[FIGURE 19a]

ENAMELED WIRE WOUND INTO COIL

TAPE

SANDPAPER THE ENDS OF THE WIRE.

SUPPORTS

[FIGURE 19b]

THUMBTACKS

[FIGURE 19c]

COIL

MAGNET

D-CELLS

BATTERY HOLDER

INSULATED WIRES

19a) Make a coil by winding 30 cm of enameled wire around a ruler. Use sandpaper to remove the enamel from the ends of the wire. b) Make supports for the coil from two 10-cm (4-in) pieces of bare copper wire or paper clips. Use thumbtacks to hold the supports in place on a small piece of soft pine board. c) Connect two D-cells to the supports and give the coil a slight push to start it spinning over the magnet.

Next, make supports for the coil using bare 20-gauge copper wire (or paper clips) and thumbtacks, as shown in Figure 19b. Use thumbtacks to hold the supports upright on a small length of a soft pine board. Put the two bare ends of the wires extending from the coil through the loops of the supports. Place a magnet beneath the coil. Use insulated wires to connect two thumbtacks to a two-D-cell battery, as shown in Figure 19c. If a two-cell holder is not available, two one-cell battery holders can be connected with a wire. Give the coil a little flip with your fingers and watch your motor spin.

Will the motor work if you use only one D-cell? What can you do to make the motor turn faster? What can you do to make the motor turn the other way? Can you use two magnets and make the motor turn? If so, where should you place the magnets?

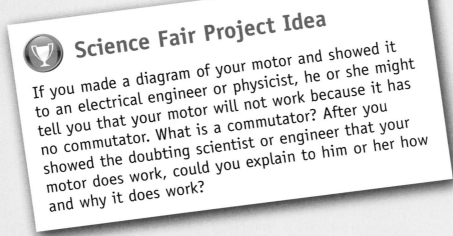

Science Fair Project Idea

If you made a diagram of your motor and showed it to an electrical engineer or physicist, he or she might tell you that your motor will not work because it has no commutator. What is a commutator? After you showed the doubting scientist or engineer that your motor does work, could you explain to him or her how and why it does work?

Materials:
- small nail
- 2 plastic cups
- monofilament fishing line
- paper clips
- tape measure
- garden hoses
- 2 large metal funnels

You can build your own private-line toy telephone. Use a small nail to make a hole in the bottom of each of the cups. Then thread the ends of a long piece of monofilament fishing line through the holes. Tie the ends of the line to paper clips inside the cups. That way the line will stay connected and can be made taut. Each cup serves as both transmitter and receiver. Use your toy telephone to carry on a conversation with a friend who will speak into and listen through the other cup.

What is the maximum range of your telephone? What other materials can you use as "telephone lines"? Does the tautness of the line affect the transmission of sound? If so, how does it affect transmission? Does the frequency of the sound affect transmission—that is, are low-frequency sounds, such as thunder, heard better than those with a high frequency, such as squeaks?

You can also make a toy telephone system by joining two or more garden hoses. As you speak softly into one end of the hose, have a friend listen with his or her ear against the other end. When your friend speaks into the other end of the hose, can you hear him or her?

Is the transmission of sound improved if you put a funnel into the end of the hose into which you speak? Is sound transmission improved if you put a funnel into the end of the hose where you listen? Is the transmission of the sounds affected by their frequencies? If so, how is it affected?

How could you arrange the hoses so that they could become an intercom system for your home?

Science Fair Project Ideas

- Investigate how a real telephone works.
- How do dolphins and other water mammals use echolocation to locate objects? Is there any evidence to indicate that these mammals communicate with one another?

Materials:
- pencil
- thin cardboard
- pencil sharpener
- ruler
- wire cutters
- drawing compass
- scissors
- smooth, level surface, such as a tabletop
- a friend
- stopwatch or a watch or clock with a second hand
- pencil or pen
- notebook

Newton's first law of motion tells us that a moving object will continue moving with a constant velocity unless a force acts on it. In much the same way, a spinning top will keep on spinning unless a force is applied to it.

You can make a toy top of your own from a pencil and some disks made of thin cardboard. To begin, sharpen the pencil, but do not make it too sharp. The end of the pencil lead should be about a millimeter in diameter. Use wire cutters to cut off the pencil so that it is about 6 cm (2.5 in) long.

Use a drawing compass to make circles about 8 cm (3 in) in diameter on thin cardboard, as shown in Figure 20a. Cut out cardboard disks with scissors and mark their exact centers with a pencil.

On a smooth, level surface, try to make the pencil spin by itself. Next, make a more conventional toy top by pushing the pencil point straight through the center of one of the disks. The point of the pencil should extend about 2 cm (0.75 in) below the bottom of the disk (see Figure 20b).

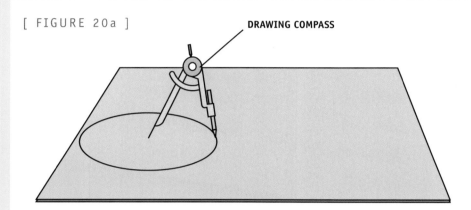

[FIGURE 20a]

DRAWING COMPASS

[FIGURE 20b]

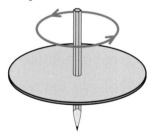

20a) Use a drawing compass to mark circles on a piece of thin cardboard.
b) Make a toy top from the disks and a short length of pencil.

Set this top spinning on the smooth surface. Ask a friend to use a stopwatch or a watch or clock with a second hand or mode to measure the time the disk keeps spinning before its edge hits the surface. Do this ten times and determine the average length of time the top spins.

Do you think the mass of the disk has any effect on the time that the top spins? To find out, add a second cardboard disk to the top. Again, measure the spin time for ten spins and calculate the average spin time.

What do you think will happen to the spin time if you add a third disk to your top? Try it! Were you right?

Science Fair Project Ideas

- Does the position of the mass affect the top's spin time? Will a disk with most of its mass farther from the pencil's shaft spin longer than one with the mass close to the pencil? Design and carry out experiments to find out.
- Investigate the laws of conservation of momentum and conservation of angular momentum. How are these laws related to a spinning top?

Chapter 4

Balloons, Balls, Bounces, and Spins

HOPEFULLY, YOU HAD FUN PLAYING WITH THE TOYS YOU BUILT IN CHAPTER 3. In this chapter, you will be using balloons and balls to learn about science. You probably associate balloons with parties, and balls with such sports as basketball, tennis, softball, baseball, football, lacrosse, and golf. However, balloons and balls can also be used to investigate electricity, pressure, expansion and contraction of gases, elasticity, curveballs, and strange bounces that result from a combination of spin and friction.

Materials:

- balloons
- string
- clear plastic tape
- ruler
- table
- puffed rice cereal
- bowl
- various other dry cereals
- Ping-Pong ball

Electrical charges dissipate (or leak away) quickly in warm, damp air; consequently, you should do this experiment on a winter day or a day when the humidity is low.

Long ago, scientists found that there are two kinds of charge, which they called positive and negative. It was Benjamin Franklin, one of the men who signed the Declaration of Independence, who established definitions of positive and negative charge. He defined glass that had been rubbed with silk, or anything repelled by the glass, to be positively charged. A rubber rod rubbed with wool, or any- thing repelled by the rubber rod, was said to have a negative charge. What kind of charge—positive or negative—do you think the silk had after it was used to rub the glass? What kind of charge do you think the wool had after it was used to rub the rubber?

You will find the answer to those questions and others in this experiment.

Blow up a balloon and hang it from a string. You can give the balloon a charge by rubbing it on your hair. After you have rubbed the balloon, what happens when you bring your hair near the balloon?

Now hang a second balloon from a string so that the two balloons hang side by side. Rub both balloons on your hair so that you give them both the same kind of charge. What do you notice about the balloons? Do they attract or repel each other? Do like charges attract or repel?

Charged Up

Was the charge on your hair, which you used to charge the balloon, the same or opposite of the charge on the balloon? How do you know?

You can charge two plastic strips of tape and determine the charge on each one. First, suspend a balloon from a string. Tape the end of the string to a door frame so that the balloon hangs freely. Next, charge the balloon by rubbing it on your hair. Then tear off two 15-cm (6-in) strips of clear plastic tape. Fold one end of each strip so that you can grip the tape without having it adhere to your skin. Stick one strip of tape to the top of a clean table. Stick the second strip on top of the first one. Holding only the folded part of the bottom strip, pull both pieces of tape off the table. Then use the folded ends to pull the two strips apart quickly.

Slowly bring first one strip and then the other close to the balloon. Do the strips carry the same or opposite charges? How do you know? How could you determine the sign (+ or −) of the charge on each strip?

Just for fun, pour a few pieces of puffed rice cereal into a bowl. Charge a balloon and hold it over the cereal. What happens? Since the puffed rice has not been charged, how can you explain what you observe?

Can you use a charged balloon to move other kinds of cereal? How can you use a charged balloon to make a Ping-Pong ball roll without touching it?

 Science Fair Project Ideas

- Investigate electrostatic induction. What is it? How is it related to what you observed with the puffed rice and the charged balloon? Design experiments to demonstrate electrostatic induction.
- Investigate static charge as opposed to moving charge (current). How do they differ? How are each produced?

Materials:

- 2 balloons
- two 1- or 2-liter glass or rigid plastic bottles
- refrigerator and freezer
- pan of hot water

Pull the neck of a balloon over the mouth of each of two empty 1- or 2-liter glass or rigid plastic bottles. (The bottle must be hard plastic, not the soft plastic in ordinary soda bottles.) Put one bottle in the refrigerator. Put the other bottle in a pan of hot water.

Watch what happens to the balloon on the bottle that was placed in hot water. What do your observations tell you? What effect does temperature have on the volume of a gas?

After a few minutes, predict what the balloon on the bottle you put in the refrigerator will look like. Then, open the refrigerator and look. What has happened to the balloon? Does what you observe agree with your prediction?

Put the bottle and balloon that was in the hot water in a freezer. What do you think will happen to the balloon? What do you think will happen to the balloon on the bottle that was in the refrigerator if you place the bottle in hot water?

🏆 Science Fair Project Idea

Design and carry out an experiment to find out by what fraction of its original volume a gas expands or contracts with each degree-Celsius change in temperature.

4.3 A Balloon in a Bottle or a Rocket Launcher?

Materials:

- an adult
- balloon
- rigid plastic bottle (pint-size)
- nail or drill to make a hole in the bottle
- unsharpened pencil

Place all but the mouth of a balloon inside a rigid plastic bottle. (The bottle must be hard plastic, not the soft plastic in ordinary soda bottles.) Pull the mouth of the balloon over the opening at the top of the bottle, as shown in Figure 21. Try to inflate the balloon by blowing into it. Why can't you fill the balloon with air?

Ask an adult to punch or drill a hole in the side of the bottle near its bottom. Now you will find that you can inflate the balloon. Why can you inflate the balloon now that the bottle has a hole in it?

Inflate the balloon and then put your thumb over the hole near the bottom of the bottle. As you can see, the balloon remains inflated even when you remove your mouth from the balloon. How can the balloon remain inflated when its mouth is open to the air?

Can you use the balloon as a "rocket launcher"? Blow up the balloon, and then put your thumb firmly over the hole in the bottle. Keeping your head away from the bottle, put an unsharpened pencil into the balloon. Continue to keep your head away from the bottle as you remove your thumb. Does the balloon contract and launch the pencil into the air?

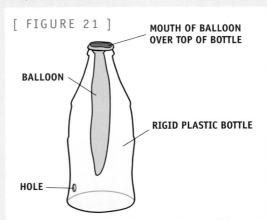

[FIGURE 21]

MOUTH OF BALLOON OVER TOP OF BOTTLE

BALLOON

RIGID PLASTIC BOTTLE

HOLE

You can blow up the balloon in the bottle only if there is a hole in the bottle.

Materials:
- one-hole rubber stopper
- 2 identical balloons
- twist tie

Blow up a balloon, attach its neck over one end of the stopper, and seal off the balloon with a twist tie. Attach an uninflated balloon to the other side of the stopper. The two balloons can now be connected through the hole in the stopper once you remove the twist tie (see Figure 22).

What do you think will happen when you remove the twist tie so that air can flow between the two balloons? Would you predict that the air will move from the large balloon into the small one until the two balloons are equal in size?

You might be surprised to see that when you open the passage between the two balloons, nothing happens. Why do you think that air does not flow from the large balloon to the smaller one?

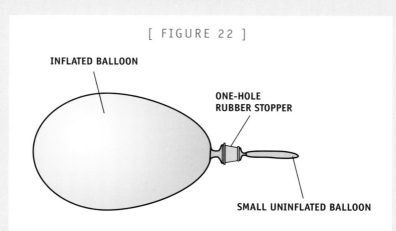

[FIGURE 22]

INFLATED BALLOON

ONE-HOLE
RUBBER STOPPER

SMALL UNINFLATED BALLOON

What is mysterious about this connected pair of balloons?

Balloons

Think about how hard it is to force the first few milliliters of air into a balloon. Once you have partially filled the balloon, it is much easier to blow air into it. Since pressure is related to radius, the pressure of the air in a balloon that has a small radius (partially inflated) is greater than the pressure in a balloon with a large diameter (fully inflated). The greater pressure inside the partially inflated balloon makes it harder to blow more air into it.

Science Fair Project Idea

Design an experiment to measure the pressure of the air in a balloon. Measure the pressure at various balloon diameters, and then plot a graph of pressure versus balloon diameter. How can you find the approximate volume of the air in a balloon by measuring its diameter? If you release the air in a balloon, will the air occupy more or less space than it did in the balloon?

Materials:
- beach ball
- calm day, or a basement, garage, or room where there is plenty of open space
- baseball or softball pitcher
- baseball or softball
- tennis ball and racquet
- basketball

A beach ball is easily moved by the wind. If you do this experiment outside, it should be done on a very calm day. If you do it inside, it should be done in the basement, garage, or a room where there is plenty of open space.

Hold the beach ball in both hands and launch it forward without any spin. The ball will travel in a straight line, but will, of course, fall to the floor.

Next, launch the ball forward, but give it a clockwise spin as seen by you (Figure 23a). Repeat the experiment several times and watch the ball carefully. Does it curve to the right or to the left as it moves forward?

Now launch the ball so that it has a counterclockwise spin (Figure 23b). Do this several times. Which way does the ball curve now?

If you hold the ball with the tips of your fingers, you can launch it with backspin, as shown in Figure 24a. This will affect the way it bounces. Can you give it enough backspin to make it bounce back toward you after it hits the floor?

Can you predict what will happen if you launch the ball with topspin, as shown in Figure 24b? Try it! Were you right?

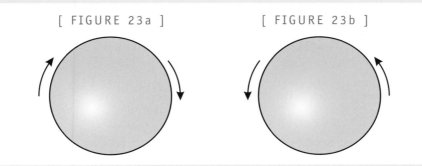

[FIGURE 23a]   **[FIGURE 23b]**

The arrows show the direction of rotation as seen by a person who launches a ball with a) clockwise spin and b) counterclockwise spin.

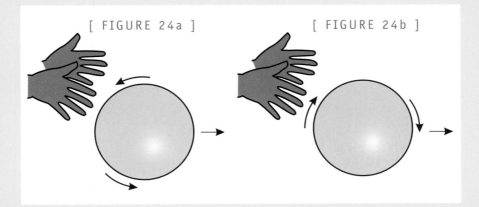

[FIGURE 24a]   **[FIGURE 24b]**

The ball is launched forward as seen from the side. a) The ball is launched with backspin. b) The ball is launched with topspin.

Ask a baseball or softball pitcher how he or she throws a curveball. Do they apply a spin to the ball? Watch him or her throw one. Does the ball they throw curve the way you would predict on the basis of the experiments you have done?

Can you make a tennis ball curve by hitting it with a racquet so that it spins clockwise or counterclockwise? Can you make a basketball bounce differently by applying backspin or topspin?

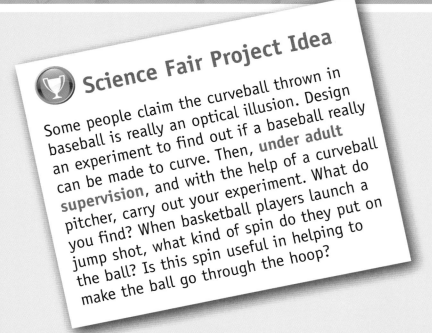

Science Fair Project Idea

Some people claim the curveball thrown in baseball is really an optical illusion. Design an experiment to find out if a baseball really can be made to curve. Then, **under adult supervision**, and with the help of a curveball pitcher, carry out your experiment. What do you find? When basketball players launch a jump shot, what kind of spin do they put on the ball? Is this spin useful in helping to make the ball go through the hoop?

4.6 The Way the Ball Bounces

Materials:

- an adult
- a partner
- different kinds of balls: e.g., tennis, golf, baseball, rubber, Ping-Pong, marble, clay, Superball
- yardstick or meterstick
- different surfaces: e.g., wood floor, concrete, tile, newspaper, and carpeting
- wooden board balanced on two bricks or blocks
- freezer
- cookie sheet
- oven
- tongs, large forceps, or pot holders

You will find this experiment a lot easier to do if you have someone help you. One person can drop the ball while the other watches to see how high it bounces.

Drop a ball from a height of 90 cm (36 in) onto a hard floor. How high does it bounce? You will have to get your head down beside the yardstick or meterstick to see how high the bottom of the ball rises. Why should you always make your measurements from the bottom of the ball? (*Hint*: How far does the ball actually fall and rise?)

What fraction of its original height does the ball attain after its first bounce? After its second bounce?

If you drop the ball from the height to which it rose after its first bounce, can you predict how high it will bounce this time? Can you predict how high it will bounce if you drop it from a height of 46 cm (18 in)? Of 30 cm (12 in)?

Try dropping other kinds of balls onto the same surface. Which kind of ball is the bounciest? Which one is the least bouncy? (Did you try a ball of clay?) Which ball do you think will keep bouncing for the longest time?

Do you think the kind of surface on which the balls land will have any effect on their bounce heights? To find out, try the same experiment on different surfaces such as concrete, tile, newspaper, and carpeting. What do you find? Can you explain your results?

You may find it helpful, as you think about your results, to try dropping a ball on a firm wooden floor and then on a piece of wood balanced on two bricks or blocks.

To see if temperature has any effect on a ball's bounciness, first see how high the different balls bounce at room temperature. Then place the balls in a freezer (or outdoors if it is very cold) for about an hour. Remove the balls one at a time and test their bounciness. Has the lower temperature changed the bounciness of any of the balls?

Can you predict what will happen to the bounciness of the balls if they are heated?

Ask an adult to help you test your predictions by placing the balls on a cookie sheet and heating them in a warm (not hot) oven for a few minutes.

When the balls are warm, use tongs, forceps, or pot holders to remove them from the oven one at a time and test each ball for bounciness.

Are any of the balls bouncier than before? If they are, do they retain their bouncier nature after they cool?

If you have not tried it yet, roll a piece of clay into a ball and drop it. Examine the clay carefully after it has fallen. Compare its shape with that of the other balls you dropped. Can you explain why the clay behaved differently?

What can you do to make a ball bounce higher than the height from which it is released? Is it easier to do this for some balls than for others? Are there any for which this is impossible?

Materials:

- an adult
- stopwatch (optional) or clock or watch with a second hand
- ball
- meterstick, yardstick, or tape measure
- notebook
- pencil or pen
- height of 4 m, or 13 ft 1 in (such as a second-story window) from which to drop a ball
- graph paper
- piece of heavy string about 3 m (10 ft) long
- heavy spike or bolt
- 4 heavy washers or nuts
- concrete floor or wide board (if experiment is done on a non-concrete floor)
- paper clips
- ladder, stool, or step ladder

A falling object changes speed as it falls. When you release it, its speed is zero, so its speed must increase. But how? Does it suddenly reach a constant speed and then fall at that rate? Or does its speed gradually increase as it falls—that is, does it accelerate as it falls? To find out, you can use a stopwatch or make a rough measurement of the time for a ball to fall different distances by quickly counting to five ("one, two, three, four, five"). It should take about one second to count rapidly to five. Test this time measurement by counting to five as fast as you can ten times. It should take 10 seconds. You can check this by using a stopwatch or clock or watch with a second hand to measure the time as you count. Adjust your counting speed to get it right. If a count of five takes 1 second, each count corresponds to 1/5 second (0.2 second).

Hold the ball 1 m (3 ft 3 in) above the floor. Start the stopwatch or begin counting the instant you release the ball. Stop the watch or stop counting at the moment the ball strikes the floor. Record your results in a notebook. Repeat your measurements several times until your measurements are consistent. (It takes a few tries to get the hang of starting and stopping the watch or count.) Next, drop the ball from a height of 2 m (6 ft 6 3/4 in). If the ball falls at a steady speed, it should take twice as long to fall 2 m as it did to fall 1 m. How long does it take for the ball to fall 2 m? Does it take the ball twice as long or less than twice as long to fall 2 m? What does this tell you?

Ask an adult to help you measure the time for a ball to fall 4 m (13 ft 1 in). Dropping the ball from a second-story window will probably provide the height you need. How long does it take the ball to fall 4 m? Is this twice the time it took to fall 2 m? Is it four times the time it took the ball to fall 1 m? What do these measurements tell you? Do you think the ball falls at a steady speed, or do you think it accelerates (increases its speed)? Why?

Suppose you find that the times for a ball to fall different distances are similar to the results shown in Table 1.

Data like those in Table 1 suggest that the ball accelerates as it falls. In fact, the data indicate that when the time doubles, the ball falls not twice as far but four times as far. (Notice that the time to fall 4 m was only twice as long as the time to fall 1 m.) The square of a number is that number multiplied by itself. For example, 3 squared (3×3, or 3^2) is 9. Study Table 1 and try to find a relationship between distance fallen and time to fall.

TABLE 1.

Times for a ball to fall different distances

Distance fallen (meters)	Time to fall (seconds)
1.0	0.45
2.0	0.65
3.0	0.78
4.0	0.90

Is it possible that the distance fallen is proportional to the square of the time to fall?

One way to test this idea is to plot a graph with distance (d) on the vertical axis and the square of the time (t^2) on the horizontal axis. You can do this very easily. In a notebook, record the data shown in Table 1, leaving room for a third column in which you record the square of the time. For example, the square of 0.45 s is 0.20 s^2. Next, plot the data for distance (on the vertical axis) versus time squared (horizontal axis) on your graph. Do the same for the data you collected. What do you conclude?

Can you see from your graph that the distance fallen is proportional to the square of the time to fall?

You can build a device to see whether or not objects fall through distances that are related as the squares of their times to fall. Tie one end of a piece of heavy string about 3 m (10 ft) long around a heavy spike or bolt. Slide four heavy washers or nuts to serve as weights onto the string and let them slide down to the spike or bolt. **Have an adult** help you tie the other end of the string to something at least 2.4 m (about 8 ft) above a concrete floor. (If the experiment is done on a different type of floor such as one in a house or school, place the spike or bolt on a wide board so that you will not damage the floor.) Use paper clips to support the washers or nuts at heights of 15 cm, 60 cm, 135 cm, and 240 cm (6 in,

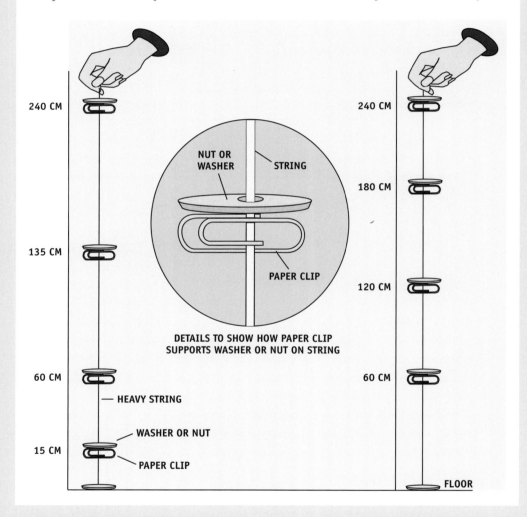

240 CM

135 CM

60 CM

15 CM

HEAVY STRING

WASHER OR NUT

PAPER CLIP

240 CM

180 CM

120 CM

60 CM

FLOOR

NUT OR WASHER　STRING

PAPER CLIP

DETAILS TO SHOW HOW PAPER CLIP
SUPPORTS WASHER OR NUT ON STRING

25a) If height of fall is related to the square of the time to fall, then washers dropped from height ratios of 1:4:9:16 should strike the floor at equal time intervals if released simultaneously. b) If height of fall is directly related to the time to fall (constant speed while falling), then washers dropped from height ratios of 1:2:3:4 should strike the floor at equal time intervals.

24 in, 53 in, and 95 in) above the bolt or spike resting on the floor, as shown in Figure 25a. As you can see, the heights of the second, third, and fourth weights are 4, 9, and 16 times as high as the first weight is above the floor or board. Consequently, the heights of the weights that will fall to the floor are, relative to the height of the first weight, in the ratios of 4:1, 9:1, and 16:1. If the heights that objects fall really are related to the squares of the times required to fall, you should hear the weights hit the floor at equal time intervals when the **adult** releases the top of the string. What do you hear when this happens? Based on what you hear, does the height through which an object falls appear to be related to the square of the time?

On the other hand, if objects fall at a constant speed, the heights of fall should be in the same ratio as the times to fall because at constant speed an object travels twice as far in twice the time. To test this idea, support the washers or nuts at 60-cm (2-ft) intervals, as shown in Figure 25b. When the **adult** releases the string and these weights fall, do they hit the floor at equal time intervals?

Science Fair Project Idea

Italian physicist Galileo (1564–1642) approached the problem of timing falling objects in another way. He "diluted gravity" by having balls roll down an inclined plane instead of falling freely. Why did he call it "diluting gravity"? See whether you can devise a way to dilute gravity in order to measure the times required for objects to "fall" through different heights. Do you think a heavy ball falls at a faster rate than a lighter one? Design an experiment of your own to find out.

Chapter 5

Projectiles, Swings, Slides, Seesaws, and More!

THERE ARE LOTS OF EXPERIMENTS THAT CAN BE DONE on a playground, an athletic field or court, a lawn, or a vacant lot. As you will see, some of the experiments you can do on a playground are closely related to smaller-scale experiments you can do in your kitchen. Remember that not everyone goes to a playground to do experiments; many people go there just to play and have fun. Don't let your fun in doing experiments interfere with their fun in playing. If your friends ask what you are doing, they may be interested in science, too. Perhaps they will like to help you with your investigations.

Materials:

- hallway or level sidewalk
- tennis ball
- chalk
- balloon
- water
- bicycle
- paper and pencil
- 2 large marbles
- flat ruler
- 2 identical coins
- table
- grooved ruler
- small board
- tacks
- hammer
- small blocks of wood
- box
- sheets of cardboard
- paper
- transfer or carbon paper (available at craft, art, or woodworking stores)
- partner
- tape
- lawn hose or high-powered squirt gun
- protractor
- level surface, such as a stand, garden table, or seesaw frame
- tape measure

If you ride your bike at a steady speed along a level sidewalk, you move horizontally at a steady speed. If you drop a ball, it falls straight down to the ground. But what happens if you drop a ball while you are moving? Does the ball continue to move forward as it falls? Does it fall faster than a ball that is dropped from rest?

To begin this investigation, walk along a level sidewalk carrying a tennis ball in your hand. Release the ball and continue walking. Does the ball continue to move forward with you as it falls and rebounds so that you can catch it as you continue to walk? Or does the ball remain where you dropped it so that you have to stop to catch it? What happens if you stop walking at the moment you drop the ball? Does the ball bounce up where you can catch it, or does it bounce on ahead of you?

Another way to answer this question is to make a bull's-eye with chalk on a level walk or driveway. Then make a water "bomb" by filling a balloon with water and tying off the neck. Ride your bike over the bull's-eye as you carry the water-filled balloon in your hand. Release the water bomb when it is directly over the bull's-eye. Does the bomb "explode" on the bull's-eye, or does it continue to move and land ahead of the bull's-eye beside your moving bicycle?

What can you conclude about the motion of a falling object that was moving horizontally when it began to fall? Draw what you believe was the path of the water bomb or the tennis ball that you dropped while moving horizontally.

Does an object that is moving horizontally fall faster, slower, or at the same rate as one that is dropped from rest? To find out, you can do some experiments in your home.

Carefully support two large marbles between your thumb and index finger, as shown in Figure 26a. Use one finger of your other hand to project one of the marbles horizontally. Because contact between the two marbles is holding them in place, if one is sent off in a horizontal direction, the other will fall. Listen carefully. Do the two marbles hit the floor at the same time, or does one land before the other?

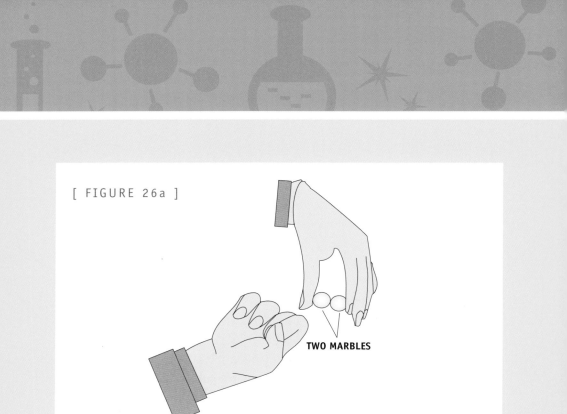

[FIGURE 26a]

TWO MARBLES

[FIGURE 26b]

FINGER HOLDS RULER
FIRMLY AGAINST
TABLE TOP.

FLAT RULER

COIN WILL BE PROJECTED
HORIZONTALLY AS IT FALLS.

TABLE

COIN WILL FALL STRAIGHT
DOWN TO FLOOR.

Does an object that is falling horizontally fall at the same rate as one
that falls straight down? a) One way to find out is to use two marbles.
b) Another way to find out is to use two coins.

Another way to do this experiment is shown in Figure 26b. Place a ruler on the edge of a table, as shown. Put one coin on the table and the other coin on the end of the ruler that is hanging off the table. Use your finger to hold the ruler firmly against the table top. Strike the edge of the ruler sharply at the point and in the direction indicated by the arrow. The coin resting on the ruler will fall straight down to the floor; the coin on the table will be projected horizontally. Again, listen carefully. Do the two coins hit the floor at the same time, or does one land before the other? What can you conclude about the rate of fall of the two objects?

THE PATH OF A PROJECTILE

To see if your drawing of the path of a falling object that is also moving horizontally is similar to an actual path, you can map the path of a marble in such a fall. To do this, let a marble roll down a grooved ruler as shown in Figure 27. The ruler is fastened to a small board with tacks hammered into the board. It is curved to make a ramp by placing a block of wood under the ruler as shown. The grooved-ruler launcher is put on a level, elevated surface so that the marble can fall as it moves horizontally after leaving the end of the ruler. A sheet of cardboard next to the front of the end of the ruler will allow you to map the marble's path.

Always start the marble at the top of its "launching pad." A sheet of carbon paper placed facedown over a sheet of white paper can be used to mark the landing point of the marble. Mark the landing point and the point where the marble leaves the ruler on the vertical sheet of cardboard. With a pencil, make a rough sketch of the path you think the marble follows during its flight. Compare the sketch with the actual path by watching the marble from the side as it travels from the end of the ruler to the point where it lands. It will help if a partner releases the marble at the top of the launching ramp while you watch its flight through the air from the side. Keep watching, launching, and mapping until you have drawn a path that matches the path followed by the marble. You will know you have succeeded when the marble, in its flight, follows the path marked on the cardboard sheet.

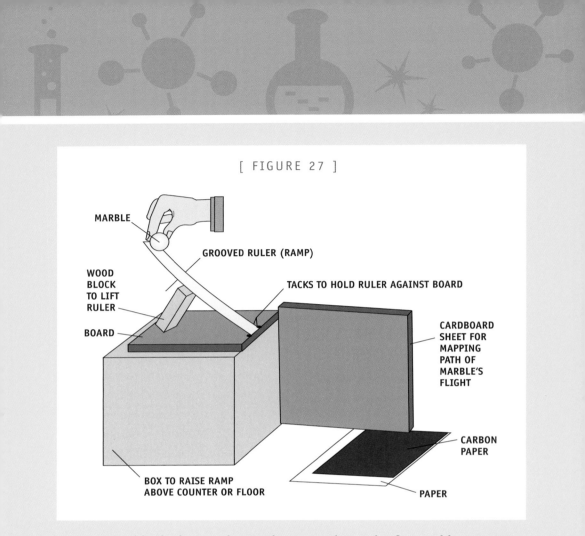

[FIGURE 27]

MARBLE

GROOVED RULER (RAMP)

WOOD
BLOCK
TO LIFT
RULER

TACKS TO HOLD RULER AGAINST BOARD

BOARD

CARDBOARD
SHEET FOR
MAPPING
PATH OF
MARBLE'S
FLIGHT

CARBON
PAPER

BOX TO RAISE RAMP
ABOVE COUNTER OR FLOOR

PAPER

**This device can be used to map the path of a marble
projectile launched from a grooved-ruler ramp.**

If you have difficulty, rest another sheet of cardboard horizontally
on blocks at different levels below the end of the ruler. By placing carbon
paper on white paper taped to the horizontal cardboard, you can mark
the position where the marble lands at different points along its flight
to the floor or counter. These points can then be marked on the vertical
sheet of cardboard.

How will the path of the marble change if you raise the top end of
the ramp upward? If you lower the top end of the ramp downward?

WATER PROJECTILES

You can take these experiments with projectiles (objects that are projected so that they move both vertically and horizontally) back to the playground or lawn. There you can use a lawn hose or a high-powered squirt gun (that uses compressed air) to launch water missiles in rapid sequence. In addition to seeing the path of the projectiles, you can investigate the range of these projectiles when they are launched into the air at different angles.

Use a sheet of cardboard to build a large half-protractor as shown in Figure 28. Place the giant protractor on a level surface, such as a stand, garden table, or seesaw support so that you will know the angle at which you launch the water projectiles. Of course, speed also affects the range of projectiles, so you want to be sure the speed at which the water emerges from the water gun or hose is the same for each angle. You can do this by marking the point where the water lands when it is fired horizontally from the level surface on which you place the protractor. Test several times to be sure that point is approximately the same each time before projecting the water at different angles.

After establishing the fixed range for 0 degrees, launch the water at an angle of 10 degrees. Have a partner mark the point where the water lands. The distance from the launch site to the point where the water lands is the range for that angle. Measure and record the distance. Repeat the experiment for 20, 30, 40, 45, 50, 60, 70, 75, and 80 degrees. Why might it be wise to skip 90 degrees?

For which angle is the range greatest? Are there angles for which the range is very nearly or exactly the same? If there are, what are these angles?

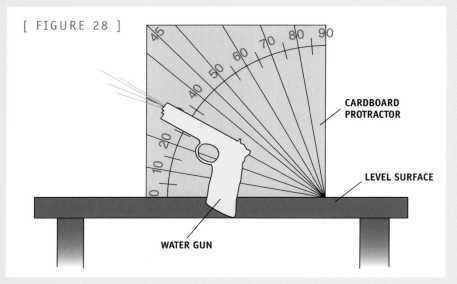

[FIGURE 28]

CARDBOARD PROTRACTOR

LEVEL SURFACE

WATER GUN

What angle of launch gives the maximum range for projectiles? This water gun is being fired at an angle of 30 degrees.

Science Fair Project Idea

Find out how falling objects accelerate as they fall. Use that information to determine how long it takes for a projectile launched from a ramp such as the one in Figure 27 to reach the floor. Use that information together with the horizontal distance the projectile travels to determine its horizontal velocity. Then use all your information to map the projectile's expected path at intervals of 0.05 seconds. Compare the map you have made with the actual path of the projectile. How closely do they agree?

Materials:

- friend
- playground swings
- stopwatch, or clock or watch with second hand
- people of very different weights
- playground slide
- waxed paper
- newspaper, brown paper, aluminum foil, plastic wrap, etc.
- seesaw (teeter-totter)
- bathroom scale with a dial

- tape measure, yardstick, or meterstick
- chalk
- 2 friends
- pencil and pad or notebook
- miniature merry-go-round, carousel, whirligig, or similar playground ride
- tennis ball
- accelerometer (see Figure 30 on page 122)
- table or counter

In the last experiment, you probably realized that the playground is a good place to carry out a lot of science experiments. There are slides, swings, seesaws (teeter-totters), miniature merry-go-rounds (carousels or whirligigs), and lots of space. You can experiment with all of them.

SWINGING PHYSICS: A SWING PENDULUM

Have a friend sit on a swing. He or she is to do nothing—no pumping—just sit. Give your friend a small push. Then use a stopwatch or a watch with a second hand to find out how long it takes your friend to make ten oscillations. A complete oscillation is the movement from one end of the back-and-forth motion to the other end and back again. What is the period of the swing (the time to make one complete oscillation) with your friend seated on it? Why is it more accurate to measure the time to make ten oscillations rather than just one? How can you find the period (the time to make one oscillation)?

Next, give your friend a harder push so that he or she swings through a greater distance. Again, measure the time to make ten complete oscillations. How does amplitude (distance the swing moves) affect its period?

Ask someone who is much heavier or lighter than your friend to sit on the same swing. How does the weight of the person on the swing affect the swing's period?

Finally, ask your friend to sit on a swing that is much longer (from points of support to seat) than the swing he or she was on before. Again, measure the period of the swing by timing ten oscillations. Then repeat the experiment with your friend on a swing that is much shorter than the first one you used. Does the length of a swing affect its period? If so, how is its period affected?

SLIDING PHYSICS: FRICTION ON A PLAYGROUND SLIDE

Have your friend slide down a playground slide. He or she should be able to go down the slide without having to push to get started. Use a stopwatch or quickly count from one to five to find out how long it takes your friend to go down the slide. See Experiment 4.7 ("How Does the Speed of a Falling Object Change?") to learn how you can use rapid counting to measure time.

Have your friend repeat the experiment while sitting on a large sheet of waxed paper. How does waxed paper affect the frictional force between your friend and the metal surface of the slide? How can you tell?

Repeat the experiment with your friend seated on other surfaces such as newspaper, brown paper, aluminum foil, plastic wrap, and so on. How do these surfaces affect the friction between your friend and the slide?

Design and carry out an experiment to find out how the weight of the person on the slide affects the friction between the person and the slide. Design and carry out an experiment to find out how the surface area in contact with the slide affects the friction between person and slide.

SEESAW (TEETER-TOTTER) PHYSICS

Find a seesaw that is balanced at its center point of support. Have a friend stand on a bathroom scale that is resting on a solid, level surface. Record his or her weight. Use a tape measure, yardstick, or meterstick to measure the distance from the center of the seesaw to a point about one-third of the distance out to one end. Record that distance and mark the point with chalk. Ask your friend to sit there, while another friend pushes on the other end of the seesaw to keep the beam balanced. Place the bathroom scale on the opposite side of the beam at the same distance from the center as your friend (see Figure 29). Push on the scale until your force on the scale is enough to balance your friend on the other side of the beam. How does the force you exert (shown on the scale) compare with your friend's weight?

Next, place the bathroom scale at various distances from the center of the beam. Balance your friend by pushing on the scale at each location. Make a table similar to Table 2. Record the distance and force at each location. Some sample data are given in Table 2, but your data will probably be different.

Now have your friend move to one or more new positions, such as half or two-thirds of the distance from the center to the end of the beam, and

TABLE 2.

Distance and force at each location on the seesaw

Weight of friend on the board	Friend's distance from board's center	Distance of force from board's center	Force needed to balance friend
100 lb	2 feet	2 feet	100 lb
100 lb	2 feet	3 feet	65 lb
100 lb	2 feet	4 feet	50 lb
100 lb	2 feet	5 feet	40 lb
___	___	___	___
___	___	___	___
___	___	___	___

repeat the experiment for each new position. You may have to have your friend or an adult help you push on the scale to make the beam balance for some of these trials.

Study the data carefully. Can you find a pattern in the numbers? For each set of numbers, how does the product of your friend's weight multiplied by his or her distance from the center of the board compare with the product of the force you exert and the distance of the scale from the center of the board?

Some seesaws are adjustable; you can make one side of the seesaw longer than the other side. Why would you want to make one side longer than the other?

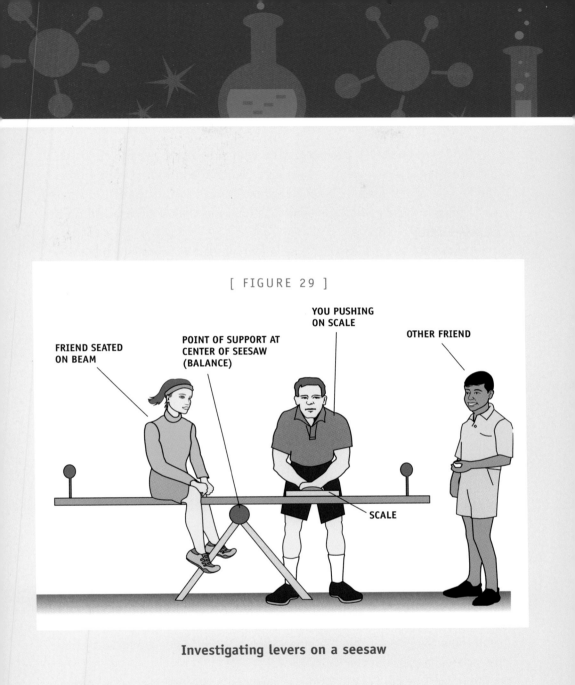

[FIGURE 29]

FRIEND SEATED
ON BEAM

POINT OF SUPPORT AT
CENTER OF SEESAW
(BALANCE)

YOU PUSHING
ON SCALE

OTHER FRIEND

SCALE

Investigating levers on a seesaw

On a seesaw that is balanced at its midpoint, where would you sit to balance someone who weighs much less than you and who is seated on the far end of the seesaw? What adjustments would you make if you wanted to balance a seesaw when someone much heavier than you is seated on the opposite side?

How could you use what you have learned on the seesaw to build a balance for weighing small objects in a laboratory?

MERRY-GO-ROUND PHYSICS

Many playgrounds have miniature merry-go-rounds, sometimes called carousels or whirligigs or other names. If you sit on the outer edge of the miniature merry-go-round while it is turning, you can experience something similar to the Coriolis effect. The Coriolis force or effect, named for the French physicist Gaspard Coriolis (1792–1843), is an apparent force that arises because we live on a spinning sphere (Earth). The path of a moving object appears to curve when it is viewed from a frame of reference that is rotating. Since Earth rotates once every 24 hours, a person on the equator moves through one full circumference (40,000 kilometers or 25,000 miles) in 24 hours. This means that a person is moving eastward at a speed of 40,000 km/24 h, which equals 1,667 km/h (about 1,000 mi/h). If the same person were standing on the North or South Pole, his or her speed would be zero, because he or she is on the axis about which Earth rotates.

A similar effect occurs on a disk rotating on a turntable. A point at the center of the disk turns but travels no distance. A point on the edge of the disk travels one full circumference with each rotation. Points between the center and the edge of the disk move at speeds that gradually increase to the maximum speed at the disk's edge.

You can see the Coriolis effect if someone kneels at the center of the merry-go-round and rolls a tennis ball toward you at the edge while you both spin slowly. What path does the ball follow on the merry-go-round floor? What path does it follow if viewed from outside the merry-go-round?

Use a tennis ball to play catch with someone seated on the opposite side of the merry-go-round when both of you are rotating slowly. Play some more catch when you are both rotating more rapidly. How can you throw the ball so that your partner can catch it? Try to play catch by rolling the ball across the merry-go-round floor. What path does the ball follow? How can you roll the ball so that your partner can catch it?

DETECTING ACCELERATION

While you may not be aware of it, you are accelerating when you ride a merry-go-round, even though you may be rotating at constant speed. The best way to detect this acceleration is to hold an accelerometer as you ride the merry-go-round. Accelerometers come in a variety of types and sizes. Figure 30 shows you how to build three different kinds.

Once you have built one or more of the accelerometers, you can do a simple experiment to see how they work. Place the accelerometer on a table or counter and move it along the surface with your hand so that its speed increases as it goes. How does each of the accelerometers you tested indicate an acceleration? How does it indicate a deceleration (a decrease in speed), or negative acceleration?

In which of the accelerometers you tested does the indicator move in the direction of the acceleration or deceleration? In which accelerometer does the indicator move in a direction that is opposite the direction of the acceleration or deceleration?

Take one or more of your accelerometers for a ride on a merry-go-round that is turning at a constant rate. According to the indicator, what is the direction of your acceleration as you ride on the merry-go-round? Does the acceleration increase or decrease as you move closer to the center of the merry-go-round? As you move farther from the center? How can you tell?

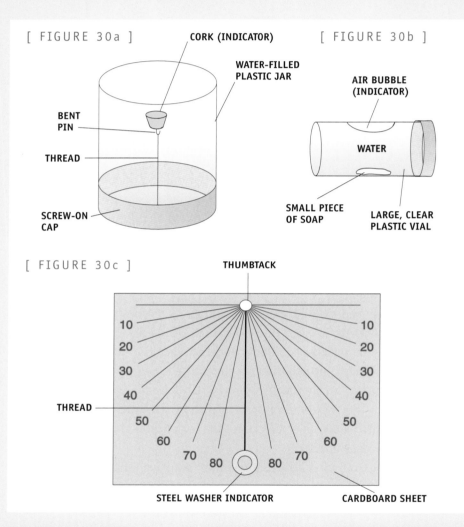

[FIGURE 30a]

CORK (INDICATOR)

WATER-FILLED
PLASTIC JAR

BENT
PIN

THREAD

SCREW-ON
CAP

[FIGURE 30b]

AIR BUBBLE
(INDICATOR)

WATER

SMALL PIECE
OF SOAP

LARGE, CLEAR
PLASTIC VIAL

[FIGURE 30c]

THUMBTACK

10   10
20   20
30   30
40   40
50   50
60   60
70   70
80 80

THREAD

STEEL WASHER INDICATOR

CARDBOARD SHEET

All of these accelerometers should be kept level or plumb when in use. In all three, the indicator gives the direction of the acceleration. a) A cork in an inverted water-filled jar is one kind of accelerometer. b) A bubble accelerometer consists of a large, clear water-filled plastic vial with enough air to make a bubble. The small piece of soap reduces surface tension so that the bubble will move more easily. c) A cardboard sheet accelerometer has a steel washer suspended from a thread supported by a thumbtack or pin.

Science Fair Project Idea

Design, build, and calibrate an accelerometer that will actually measure the magnitude (size) of accelerations. Since acceleration is change in velocity per time (acceleration = velocity change ÷ time), the accelerometer will have to be able to measure both changes in velocity, which have units such as miles per hour (mi/h) or meters per second (m/s), and time, which might be measured in seconds (s), minutes (min), or hours (h). Such an accelerometer would have numbers on it to measure accelerations in meters per second per second (m/s/s), miles per hour per second (mi/h/s), or any other units that indicate acceleration over some convenient range of values.

Materials:
- athletic friend
- sidewalk or lawn
- thick cushions
- stopwatch or watch with second hand

Many athletes say they can run faster on some fields than on others. They claim the firmness of the turf affects their speed. This experiment may provide evidence that will support or refute their claims.

Have a friend who is a good athlete stand on a sidewalk or lawn. Then ask your friend to run in place at what she or he considers a reasonably fast pace. Count the number of steps that your friend takes during a one-minute period while running on this hard surface.

After a five-minute rest, ask your friend to run in place once more at the same pace on a pair of thick cushions instead of the sidewalk or lawn. Again, count the number of steps your friend makes during a one-minute period. What happens to your friend's pace while running on the soft cushions? How do you think a soft field affects a runner's speed? Why do you think it affects his or her speed?

Science Fair Project Idea

Design an experiment to find out how running surface affects an athlete's speed. You might compare dry grass, damp grass, Astroturf, cinders, clay, macadam, and so on. On which surface do athletes seem to run fastest? What factors, other than speed, do you think should be considered in choosing the surface for an athletic field?

FURTHER READING

Books

Buttitta, Hope. *It's Not Magic, It's Science!: 50 Science Tricks that Mystify, Dazzle, and Astound!* New York: Lark Books, 2005.

Gibson, Walter B. *Fell's Official Know-It-All Guide to Advanced Magic.* Hollywood, Fla: Frederick Fell Publishers, Inc., 2000.

Moorman, Thomas. *How to Make Your Science Project Scientific, Revised Edition.* New York: John Wiley & Sons, Inc., 2002.

Pentland, Peter and Pennie Stoyles. *Toy and Game Science.* Broomall, Pa.: Chelsea House Publishers, 2003.

Smith, Alastair, Phillip Clarke, and Corinne Henderson. *The Usborne Internet-Linked Library of Science: Materials.* London, England: Usborne Publishing Ltd., 2001.

Sobey, Ed. *Inventing Toys: Kids Having Fun Learning Science.* Tucson, Ariz: Zephyr Press, 2002.

Internet Addresses

Funburst Media, LLC. *Funology. The Science of Having Fun.* 1999–2005.
<http://www.funology.com/laboratory/>

New York Hall of Science. *Try Science.* 1999–2008.
<http://tryscience.org/experiments/experiments_home.html>

Science Hound. *All Science Fair Projects.com.* 2006.
<http://all-science-fair-projects.com/>

INDEX

Gay Rights

by Tina Kafka

This book is dedicated to Zoltan, who is my greatest source of support.

© 2006 Thomson Gale, a part of The Thomson Corporation.

Thomson and Star Logo are trademarks and Gale and Lucent Books are registered trademarks used herein under license.

For more information, contact
Lucent Books
27500 Drake Rd.
Farmington Hills, MI 48331-3535
Or you can visit our Internet site at http://www.gale.com

LIBRARY OF CONGRESS CATALOGING-IN-PUBLICATION DATA

Kafka, Tina, 1950–
  Gay rights / by Tina Kafka.
      p. cm.— (Hot topics)
  Includes bibliographical references and index.
   Contents: A new civil rights movement—Gay marriage—Gay families—Gay rights in schools—Gay rights in the workplace.
   ISBN 1-59018-637-0 (hard cover : alk. paper)
   1. Gay rights—United States—Juvenile literature. I. Title. II. Series: Hot Topics
HQ76.8.U5K34 2005
323.3'264'0973--dc22
                                                                    2005005595

Printed in the United States of America